D1566396

TUNING IN

DAVID THOMAS
MATTHIEW KLINCK

TUNING IN

A JOURNALIST,
6 TRANCE CHANNELERS, AND
MESSAGES FROM THE OTHER SIDE

HAMPTON ROADS
PUBLISHING COMPANY, INC.

Cover design by Jim Warner
Cover images courtesy of Mouska Media
Interior Design by Jane Hagaman

Hampton Roads Publishing Company, Inc.
Charlottesville, VA 22906
www.hrpub.com

ISBN: 978-1-57174-646-7

Library of Congress Cataloging-in-Publication Data available
upon request

Printed in the United States of America
MV
10 9 8 7 6 5 4 3 2 1

Dedication

*To my fellow seekers,
those audacious enough to ask the Big Questions.*

Contents

Acknowledgments

First off, I'd like to thank the channelers—Lee Carroll, Wendy Kennedy, Darryl Anka, Geoffrey Hoppe, Shawn Randall, and John Cali—for being so generous with their time and so open with their hearts. Because of them, doing this project was a true pleasure.

And of course the entities that shine through them—Kryon, the Pleiadian Collective, Bashar, Tobias, Torah, and Chief Joseph—were nothing short of delightful and enlightening.

My partner on the film, Matthiew Klinck, was committed and good-humored. He must be commended for getting involved with this project at all, since we didn't know each other beforehand, and he was unfamiliar with channeling.

Eileen Cope, my literary agent at Trident Media Group, saw the movie and had the insight to believe it would make a fine book. So thank you, Eileen. I am also grateful to her assistant, Alexandra Bicks, who was very helpful.

The folks at Hampton Roads and Red Wheel/Weiser, publishers of this book, were nothing short of fantastic. I'd especially like to give a shout out to Jan Johnson, Greg Brandenburgh, and Gary Hill.

Kudos to my brothers Jeff and Ned, who helped finance the film.

Also, I'd like to mention my mom and dad, both of whom are now in spirit. Here on Earth they did the best they could with what they had and are now, I trust, reveling in the fullness of their being.

Though I don't know him personally, I thank Bruce Springsteen. I was caught in a crossfire I didn't understand, and you helped me through.

Finally, I would like to acknowledge all the seemingly random humans I've rubbed up against over the course of my life. All the girls I've kissed, the guys I've brawled with, the fellow travelers quick with a warm smile, and even the ornery cusses. I now know it has all been a perfect jigsaw puzzle, and I look forward to additional surprising pieces falling into place.

tuning in

One

Darryl Anka Channeling Bashar

If someone had told me a decade ago that I would make a documentary film about trance channelers, I would have suggested that the person was crazier than plant life.

I was a trained journalist who wore a gray cloak of skepticism, and the only thing I knew about channels was that there were lots of them on my television. I scoffed at such woo-woo nonsense, if I bothered to think about it at all.

But my crooked path did indeed lead me to make such a movie, entitled *Tuning In: Spirit Channelers in America*. And I have come to believe that channeling—higher intelligences speaking through humans—is real and happening with more frequency all over the globe.

You may think that I've drunk the Kool-Aid, that I'm just another deluded pilgrim who's lost his way and is desperately grasping at any fool thing that comes along. You would be wrong. With the aid of channeled information, I have *found* my way. The Big Questions that have blazed in me for most of my life—"Why am I here?" "Who am I?"—have been answered in delicious and satisfying ways.

I have truly come to believe that the supernatural is just the natural not yet understood. I am no scientist, and I cannot explain to you the quantum mechanics of how a spirit can speak through a biological receiver called a human. Basically, channeling involves a nonphysical entity "stepping down" energy and a person going into a trance state and "stepping up" energy, creating a melding in the middle where communication is possible.

As our evolution speeds up, as we in a sense ascend, the veil between our physical existence and the spirit world thins. Before we incarnated, we asked our non-physical friends to remind us of who we really are and to keep us on track in this tricky arena of duality. That is why more and more spirit channelers are popping up all over the globe—because we have asked for help in navigating the age we have entered, which some have termed "The Great Shift." There is a silent revolution of consciousness afoot, and more channeled information is a part of it. We are evolving quickly, and spirits are coming through to offer guidance, advice, and uncondi-tional love from a broader perspective. With our once-robust economy now anemic and many people feeling downtrodden, confused, and scared, such information couldn't be more timely.

Kryon, a highly evolved disincarnate spiritual mas-ter channeled by Lee Carroll, is well aware that skeptics abound. "Many humans," he told me, "will say, 'can't be happening. Channeling is impossible.' Yet know this: all of your spiritual texts you hold so dear have been chan-neled. This is an ancient, sacred form of communication and now here we are offering it up again. If you come to this material with an open mind and open heart, perhaps there is something to be gained from it, dear human."

It is not a stretch to say that channeled material saved my own life. Maybe that sounds hyperbolic, but a decade ago I was in full-on Hamlet mode, profoundly unhappy and neck-deep in a slow crucifixion of the spirit. Poleaxed on the twin spires of Doubt and Despair, I was drinking way too much and enjoying way too little. I was in the process of getting a bitter divorce from life itself and, to be totally honest, I wasn't long for this dusty planet. I had no money, no girlfriend, was being evicted from my Los Angeles apartment, and my hoped-for screenwriting career had fizzled on the launchpad.

I hadn't yet jammed my head in the oven, but I was desperately disconsolate. I really didn't see the point of continuing on if my existence was going to consist of mostly heartbreak and abject misery. A doctor even put me on antidepressants. They didn't work.

One Saturday afternoon I was drinking beer on the back steps of my building, wondering what it would be like to be homeless in a few days, when a bird lit on a wire directly in my line of sight, perhaps twenty feet away.

This was not a washed-out city pigeon; it was a bright-plumed white dove. Our eyes met and we stared at each other for a good minute. I felt something welling up inside me, a wave of well-being. In that moment, I knew that I wasn't alone in the universe, that I'd be okay no matter what happened. Then the bird flapped its wings and flew off toward the smoggy L.A. skyline.

My encounter with the dove wasn't exactly a burning bush, but was it a sign? I have come to believe that indeed it was. The very next day I stumbled across the *Conversations with God* books and devoured two of them right there in the bookstore. This was material channeled through Neale Donald Walsch, and I was rapt. Answers—real, cogent answers—were contained in those pages, and they were slaking my thirst like cold water to a man who'd just crawled across Death Valley. I realized I didn't even have enough money to buy the books, so I sat and sat and read and read. My stomach grumbling, I looked up and discovered that four hours had sprinted by.

I went home, got online, and began looking for more channeled material. I found plenty. Some of it had no resonance with me, and I left it behind. I came across a few channelers who seemed like outright charlatans or fakers, and of course did not revisit them.

My only criteria for continuing with a particular channeler were whether the material made sense and whether it made me *feel* the truth . . . in my heart, in my loins, in my marrow. I came back to this material again and again, finding that it not only provided answers to my questions about life, God, existence, all of it; but also offered inspiration and solace. It was a true balm, a salve.

I am, after all, trained as a journalist—a professional skeptic. So I didn't tell my friends about channeling. I was raised Catholic, so I didn't divulge anything to my family either. It wasn't that I was afraid of anyone's reaction; I just didn't want to be looked at as a weirdo. I didn't need the headache, I didn't feel like explaining; there was no reason anyone had to know.

But I did begin hearing remarks from family and friends that I looked more at peace, happier. "Just good whiskey," I'd joke.

Finally, after nearly a decade of delving into channeled material, I was struck with a thunderbolt of a thought: make a documentary about channeling. I wasn't sure where this idea even came from, so I turned the other cheek, as it were, and tried to forget about the notion.

But it persisted—a fly buzzing in my brainpan. If I did make a movie, I surmised, I would most likely have to kiss my "serious journalist" label goodbye. But I felt that I hadn't really made a mark in that field anyway. I mulled and let the idea gestate until finally one day I woke up and decided it was time to make the movie. Just like that. I simply knew the time had come.

If I had been so positively affected by profound channeled messages, I reasoned, certainly many others would benefit as well. I took the proverbial leap of faith, scooped what little money I had out of my bank account, sold my car and bought a beater, sold some gold coins, and liquidated anything else I could think of.

I'd gained a toehold in Los Angeles as a rewriter of screenplays, so I did have some friends and connections in the movie industry, people I thought might want to take this excursion with me. But their reactions were consistent and unilateral: "A movie about *channeling*? Are you crazy?"

Maybe I was, but the decision was made and I wasn't backing off. I put an ad on Craigslist for a partner, ideally someone who had cameras, professional lights, and sound equipment, and who knew how to edit. I got about twenty responses, winnowed them to a few, and met with each of them. Like in the story *Goldilocks*, the first three didn't seem just right.

But when I met the fourth, a young Canadian director named Matthiew Klinck, over a burger on a Sunday afternoon in Santa Clarita, CA, I knew we were simpatico. We had a natural rapport and within minutes were bantering like old buddies. He would later tell me: "I had this immediate connection with you, as if we'd known each other for a long time.

"But when you got into detail about this entire notion of spirit channeling, I have to admit I had flashbacks to Whoopi Goldberg in *Ghost*. But you were so passionate about it and explained it so well that my curiosity really kicked in."

By the time dessert arrived, I'd presented Matt with a simple deal memo stating that we would be partners on the project, and, to his own surprise, he found himself signing.

"No due diligence on my part, no subject research, no market research, no business plan," he now recalls with a laugh. "I basically just went on your enthusiasm and a strong hunch that I was supposed to get involved in this. You promised that you'd lined up three channelers already for interviews and you were working on three others. I didn't know you. I didn't know for sure if you were telling the truth."

Matt liked my fervor about the project, and I liked his energy, the fact that he had most of the necessary equipment and was open to the phenomenon of channeling, and that he was new to L.A. so not yet jaded. We shook hands, and only a week later we were seated in the modest home of Darryl Anka on a tree-shrouded street in the San Fernando Valley.

tuning in

Anka is a barrel-chested man with a soft voice and a smooth moon face belying his fifty-eight years. He has channeled Bashar, an extraterrestrial being from three hundred years in the future, since 1983. Bashar has come back in time to assist Earth in this period of transition, and Darryl considers him an aspect of his future self, like a great-great-great-great-great galactic grandson.

Peach-colored late November sun dappled the living room as bespectacled Darryl explained that he is certainly attuned to the fact that some people may find it difficult to believe that he's channeling an "alien."

"I always make it clear to people that they do not have to believe that Bashar is really an extraterrestrial in telepathic communication with me," he said. "If they want to believe the words are coming from another part of my own consciousness, that's fine with me. I have no way of proving Bashar's existence to anyone anyway. The most important thing is that the information, wherever it's coming from, has made a difference in many people's lives, including my own."

And mine. I had stumbled across Darryl and Bashar some seven years earlier and had an immediate, deep connection with the material. By the time I decided to make the movie, I had listened to many hours of the Bashar channelings online and on CDs, and had even attended a live seminar.

The genesis of Anka's channeling dates back nearly four decades. "On two occasions within the same week in 1973, I had close-range, broad-daylight sightings of UFOs with witnesses present both times," he said. "At each sighting we saw a dark metallic, triangular craft about thirty feet on each side. There were three blue-white lights, one on each 'point,' and one orange-red light in the center. The craft in the first sighting was about 150 feet away; in the second sighting, it was only about sixty feet away."

Anka began reading everything he could get his hands on about ETs, but he still had no clue that he would eventually be channeling one.

"Then in 1983, I went to a channeling seminar with a friend," he continued. "Not because I was fascinated by the subject, but just because he was going and it sounded interesting."

Anka found himself returning to the channeling seminars, and also listened to some on tape. "I was amazed by the consistency and quality of the information I was hearing on a variety of subjects," he says. "Eventually, that entity offered to teach channeling to whoever wished to learn. This surprised me at first, as I had assumed channeling was not something that could be taught. Nevertheless, I joined the channeling class—not intending to become a channel myself, but rather to learn more about the process by which this entity seemed capable of accessing volumes of information on endless subjects."

About midway through the classes, he said, things began to *really* get interesting. "During a guided meditation, I received what sounded like a telepathic message in my mind. I became instantly aware of three things: The message was from an extraterrestrial consciousness that I was to call 'Bashar' and the ship I had seen ten years prior was his; a memory came back to me that I had made an agreement at some point prior to this life to channel him; and now was the time to fulfill this agreement if I still felt like doing so.

"After thinking about it for a while, I decided to explore the possibility of letting this 'Bashar' entity speak through me to see what would happen. I figured that even if it wasn't really another entity—even if it was some mysterious portion of my own consciousness—the information that could be accessed through this channeling process could be used to help people make constructive and positive changes in their lives.

"Whatever the source, I decided to continue. I have now been channeling publicly since that time in 1983. Bashar has spoken on a wide variety of subjects to thousands of people throughout the United States, as well as in Japan, Australia, New Zealand, Canada, England, and Egypt."

Now it was zero hour, my favorite. Time for the channeling, to have Bashar come through and for me to ask anything. This was consistent with all six interviews Matt and I would do over the next two months: I would ask whatever I liked. None of the questions were submitted beforehand.

Darryl sat in a simple wooden chair, me seated across from him on the couch. Several cameras were set up, and Matt was wielding a handheld high-definition camera. Anka removed his wire-rimmed glasses, set them aside, cracked his knuckles, and rolled his neck a few times. He closed his eyes.

He took a deep breath. Another. Another. His face began to twitch. His breathing became deeper and deeper until it sounded almost otherworldly. His head appeared to get much heavier as his chin inched down, eventually settling on his chest. More facial tics.

I suddenly found myself very excited, my heart

hammering like a broken piston. I took a few deep, relaxing breaths of my own as Darryl continued to sink into trance state.

After about a minute of intense breathing, Darryl's head popped straight up, reanimated, and his entire body convulsed for a moment. Then a thunderclap of a voice veritably boomed: "Good morning to you in your day and time, how are you?"

> Whatever vibration you give off . . . determines, utterly and absolutely, whatever experience is reflected back to you from your reality.

Bashar's energy was so strong and vibrant that I thought my scalp might peel back. The room was now supercharged with his crisp energy. I felt invigorated and began firing my questions. I wasn't interested in knowing how my dead grandmother was doing, but rather in the Big Things: How do we create our experiences, how can we better manifest things, how can we stay healthy, what is God?

Early on, he made it clear that we are responsible for our own lives, *totally* responsible, and that nothing is being done *to* us, but rather *through* us:

≡

Whatever vibration you give off, whatever frequency you create or generate, determines, utterly and absolutely, whatever experience is reflected back to you from your reality. Because physical reality really does not empirically exist apart from your definition of it. Even your own quantum physicists are beginning to discover this. So physical reality is likened to a mirror.

Whatever it is that you give off, whatever form you give yourself, however you define and identify yourself, is what is reflected back to you from your reality, so that you can decide whether you wish to retain that idea and that frequency or whether you wish to change it.

≡

Bashar was pumped, hands cutting the air like a martial artist.

≡

From our perspective, the most effective way to alter your reality is to get in touch with, consciously, your beliefs. Find what that belief is, identify it and define it. Once you have defined the belief, you can then understand as a mechanism how it has been generating the frequency that caused the reflection you've been experiencing. You can then replace it with a belief that you prefer.

And then you can also believe, if you wish, that the new belief will replace the old one just as effectively and create reality just as effectively as the old belief did. But once you replace the belief, and thus then it generates new emotions, new thoughts, and new behaviors, you will then get a new reality that is reflective of those ideas.

≡

I wanted specifics and, since we could all use a few more dollars in the bank account, asked about money.

≡

We understand that money is one of the symbols of abundance on your planet, and that's all well and good. You can have as much money as you want. But the idea really is to relax the definition of abundance because it doesn't have to flow to you only through paper money. You open the doors through which abundance could come in all the other forms. Abundance really is simply having what you need each moment for you to do what you need to do when you need to do it.

The idea is to also examine the belief systems where you might be resistant to the idea of abundance, because many of you have belief systems unconsciously that actually keep the idea of the experience of abundance at bay. For example, you are raised on your planet with all sorts of contradictory and conflicting belief systems about money. Such as, "love of money is the root of all evil," and, "You will never be a success unless you have a lot of money." How can you allow those two things to coexist side by side without being confused?

Many people believe, "Well, I will never be successful if I don't have a lot of money." But they also believe that "I will become a greedy person, a bad person, if I get a lot of money." Many never allow themselves to become physically wealthy, because it is more important to them to be a good person than to be a bad one. So if they associate the idea of being a bad person with having a lot of money, then that's a belief they need to look at because they don't have to have that association. The idea is not that you have to become more abundant than you are. The idea is to get in touch with what you are saying you are abundant in. And if you're abundant on lack, you will experience an abundance of lack.

Again it comes down to core belief. What belief have you attached to the idea of abundance that prevents you from experiencing it in the way you would prefer to? That's the question to ask yourselves. Find out what the answers are, find out what those beliefs are that you've attached to those things, and change core beliefs.

≡

Bashar seemed like a master teacher on a roll. Some of the other entities I would encounter later were gentler, with a more overtly loving energy. Bashar was not fond of soft-pedaling; he got right to the nub of things. I certainly sensed love in the exchange, but Bashar was mostly concerned with imparting information and helping us *understand*.

I glanced at Matt and saw that he was laser-focused on shooting Darryl/Bashar—maybe slightly entranced himself. I was still feeling very energized, as if a mild electric current were running from toes to ears.

The following is most of the rest of the transcript:

≡

Q: Why you are coming through Darryl at this time?

A: An arrangement, so to speak, was made prior to the physical life of the channel within what you would call the oversoul of the channel of which I am also a part. We are part of the same soul. You may refer to me as the channel's future self and, incarnationally speaking, I would look upon the channel as my past self. Just to put it in linear terms. From your space-time perspective, the idea is that incarnations happen one after the other. But from our perspective in an other-dimensional realm we perceive all lives, all incarnations, as simultaneously concurrent. So I exist at the same time as the channel even though from another point of view you could say he is my past life and I am his future life. Thus, because we coexist simultaneously and are part of the same soul, I have the capacity to communicate with that aspect of my being that is represented by the channel's physical life.

Q: Have you ever been in human form yourself?

A: As I have just said, the physical channel sitting before you is one of my past lives on Earth. But I have other lives in other civilizations. And the idea is that I am physical in my own civilization but I have had a few human lives. Or, from our perspective, I am simultaneously having a few human lives.

Q: So, has Darryl done this before? I mean this agreement. Has he done it before?

A: There has not been a Darryl before this life. The idea is that this decision was made within the oversoul of which we are both a part. And the oversoul thus then created him and me. Projected each of our lives into physical reality in a different dimension, in a different realm. In such a manner as to facilitate what you are now experiencing as the communication you call a channeling. So that we may, from our perspective, bring through ideas and information that will aid and assist the civilization into which the channel was born in their exploration of spirituality and the growth of consciousness.

Q: In a sense, is all the channeling material coming through to remind us of something we already know?

A: Yes. All of you are spirit. All of you are eternal. All of you already know all the things that are being discussed in your so-called "new age awakening." In your spiritual investigation and exploration. This is not information that is really totally new to you as a spirit, but by being born in physical reality, by creating a physical personality, you have to some degree experienced forgetting who and what you really are. So the whole idea of exploring spirit and awakening to higher levels of consciousness is exactly as you say: a remembering, a reminding of who and what you are so that you can experience and express these higher frequency, higher level, higher consciousness ideas more consciously in physical reality and not forget any longer as you have forgotten for thousands of years.

Q: And why would we put ourselves through forgetting?

A: Because it is an experience. It is one of the valid experiences, the valid ways of experiencing reality. And really it allows you to, shall we say, go through a process that would be impossible on other levels, on higher levels. The idea is that when you create the

> *All of you are spirit. All of you are eternal. But by being born in physical reality . . . you have experienced forgetting who and what you really are.*

experience of forgetfulness and yet then, even through forgetting, still discover the idea of remembering who you are, that enhances and enriches the soul's experience of itself and adds to the overall experience of All That Is in rediscovering itself from a new perspective, a new point of view. It requires forgetting in order to have an experience of remembering and that's a valid experience within creation.

Q: In our forgetfulness there's often pain and unhappiness.

A: Yes.

Q: Why would we want to put ourselves through that?

A: It isn't that you necessarily want to put yourselves through it. But it is to some degree part and parcel of the experience of having a sense of disconnection from your true self. The idea is to learn that you don't have to do that, but you must come from a perspective of having done it in order to once again gain the experience of knowing you don't need to do it. I'll put it colloquially. You have to experience darkness in order to understand that there is light. The polarity is important in order to create an integration of polarity. Without polarity there is no integration of polarity. Again, from the perspective of All That Is, from the perspective of creation itself, it is simply a valid way of experiencing a part of itself. So it will contain polarity and experiences of polarity in order to experience gathering itself back together in an integrated way.

Q: So if someone gets cancer that person wants to put themselves through that experience on some level?

A: It isn't that the physical personality necessarily wants to have that experience. But it may be part and parcel of belief systems that have been bought into, and ideas and definitions that have been bought into, that allow you to experience the idea that you are a victim of something or out of control. But the idea is to learn through that that you're not and that you actually can create something else. That you can transmute that idea, that experience into something else or learn from it in a positive way. And the thing to also remember is that regardless of what happens to the physical personality, the spirit, the being, the consciousness is eternal and infinite and has the capacity to experience any number of things.

And even though it may experience, for a time, the idea of something that causes it pain and suffering, it is a temporary experience that the soul can nevertheless use to its benefit. Now I am not saying in any way, shape, or form that, again, this pain must be experienced. I am simply saying that it is part and parcel of the definition of the reality that you have chosen to experience, the physical time-space reality. Such things are possible in that experience, but the idea is to learn through that experience that you actually don't need to suffer. That you can remember you are creating your life and you don't have to be victim of belief systems or definitions that say you are out of control. That's the whole idea. That you can find the light and create the light even coming from forgetfulness and darkness. That shows you how powerful you are as a being, as a consciousness, as a spirit.

Q: There's a lot of talk these days about the Law of Attraction.

A: Yes. It is what we refer to as the third law.

Q: How do you describe it and explain how it works?

A: I will put it in context to the four laws that we understand that control in that sense everything within creation. From our experience there are only four laws that allow everything to be experienced, that allow everything to be created. The first law is simply that you exist. That will never change. The form may change, but the fact that you exist will never change. Existence does not become nonexistence because nonexistence is already full of the things that will never exist and there is no room in nonexistence for the things that do exist. Existence is the only quality existence has. To be. There is no "not to be."

Therefore law number one is: you exist and always will and always have. Law number two is that the one is the all and the all are the one. The whole is made up of parts. The parts are themselves aspects of the whole and each part contains the whole in a holographic way. Law number three is what you call the Law of Attraction and that simply is "what you put out is what you get back." So whatever it is that you give off, whatever form you give yourself, however you define and identify yourself, is what is reflected back to you from your reality so that you can decide whether you wish to retain that idea and that frequency or whether you wish to change it. And that leads us to the fourth law, which is change is the only constant, and everything changes except the first three laws, which never change.

Q: You say we exist and always will. If that's the case, and I believe it is, why do so many people fear death?

A: Because they have experienced the idea of disconnection from remembering that they are eternal and infinite, and thus when you don't remember that you are eternal and infinite, the physical personality ego, the construct that you create that is the physical mind, does not know that death does not equal annihilation. When the physical mind thinks that death equals nonexistence or annihilation, it then goes into survival mode. Panic, fear, doubt. But when it understands that physical reality is simply a temporary manifestation, a mask if you will, a projection of a greater consciousness that you are, and you understand that you always exist, then the fear of death vanishes.

Q: There's also a lot of talk these days about "thought creates . . . "

A: It is actually "belief creates." But we understand that sometimes these terminologies may be loosely defined on your planet and in essence it is correct that your thoughts create your reality. But on a more fundamental level it is actually your definitions and beliefs that generate the emotions that you have that generate the thoughts and actions that you also have, and all of that reinforces the reality that you're creating. But first and foremost it actually issues and originates from whatever the strongest definition or belief is that you have bought into as true.

Q: So then as we change these core beliefs and act from that, our outer reality, our lives, as it were, must change?

A: Yes, absolutely. But at first when you change a belief, because you live in a time-space reality, there might be what is called an "echo effect," and it may seem as though the outer reality hasn't changed. But the true proof that needs to occur within the individual who says they have changed their belief is not that at first the outer reality has changed to prove that they've changed their belief but that they respond to the reality differently even if it stays the same for a while. When you respond differently to the same reality, reflection, or echo than you did before, that's what proves you have changed; and when you continue to respond differently to the same reality, that will then reinforce a new frequency that will then ultimately create a new outer reality reflection.

That's how it works, and really, all it is is the simple physics of energy. That's all this is. There is no mystery to these new age ideas on your planet; when people say you create your reality, it's a matter of your thoughts, your beliefs, your behavior, your feelings. This is really just a layman's way of expressing energy physics. Again, what you put out is what you get back. For every action there is an equal and opposite reaction. It's just physics but taken to a new, deeper level of understanding with consciousness also being added into the equation. Because consciousness is what creates your experience. There is no real empirical outer reality. The only thing that is, shall we say, *real*, is your experience of it.

Q: Sometimes it's difficult to get from one place to something you would prefer . . .

A: Yes. Well again the difficulty may come from harboring beliefs that you may not even be consciously aware of and getting in touch with what those beliefs are that may be preventing you from experiencing a life of joy. But the idea is that concurrently with investigating your deepest beliefs to unlock from them, is the idea that acting on your joy whenever it might show itself, acting on your passion at every opportunity, is what will also strengthen your ability to move forward in that direction. Because passion, excitement, joy, love, that sensation in the body, that excitement in the body, that sense of balance and peace in the body, is the body's physical translation of the vibratory frequency that represents your true, natural, core, original self. The self you were actually created by creation to be.

So anytime you act on your passion to the best of your ability, every chance you get, you are then making a statement, a commitment to be harmoniously aligned with your true natural core vibration. And when you are thus functioning and staying in a state of being that is representative of your true natural core vibration, then the universe is capable of supporting anything that is representative of that true natural core vibration. But when you buy into belief systems that are out of alignment, out of sync with your natural self, and thus feel the energy as doubt, fear, hate, and so forth, judgment in that negative sense, and so forth, then the universe can only support what vibration you are giving off. And if you are giving off a vibration of being out of alignment, it can only then present to you opportunities to continue to be out of alignment. Because what you say goes. That's why you were given free will.

You are the absolute and ultimate determiner of what kind of reality experience you have. We have often said also that one of the greatest gifts that you have been given by creation—and we know this will sound funny at first in your language, but bear with us. One of the greatest gifts that you have been given by creation is that life is meaningless. What we mean by that is this: Nothing, no situation and no circumstance, actually has built-in meaning. It's neutral, devoid of meaning; it's a prop. It's a symbol. It's a representation of a concept. But the meaning you give it, automatically, unconsciously or consciously, the meaning you assign, the definition you assign to any given neutral situation is exactly what determines the effect you will get out of that situation. All situations are neutral and can serve double duty. They can create for you a negative or a positive reflection. That is solely determined by what energy, vibration, and belief system and definition you assign to that situation.

So no matter what anybody else's intention in any given circumstance might be toward you, if you assign a positive definition to that given same circumstance and situation, then you will only receive a positive effect out of that circumstance no matter what anyone else experiences. Again, the third law: What you put out is what you get back. And since every single individual really *is* their own reality, their own universe, then what you say in your universe goes. And you don't have to agree with what other people might offer as an alternative belief if you don't prefer to buy into that belief. You won't have the same experience they do in the very same situation. Again this is simple physics.

Q: It seems to be then that people are unhappy and sort of pinched off from the divine because they're not aware of how powerful they truly are?

A: In a sense, although you can never really be separated from All That Is or the "divine" as you call it, but you can create an experience as if you are separated from the divine. But since you are part of creation, you can't really be separated from it. But you can have an experience that you are. And creation supports whatever choice you make unconditionally. You are unconditionally loved, unconditionally supported, in any choice that any one of you make. Thus if you choose to believe that you are cut off and separated and choose to experience the idea of that separation, All That Is or creation can only support you in that and can only provide you with more opportunities to reinforce what you say is your choice. So it's really up to you to get in touch with why you might be choosing those things and change the beliefs that make it seem as if for some reason that's a logical choice to make when in fact it may not really be serving you.

Q: So if a person is depressed or even in despair, it's because they consider themselves separate or are cutting themselves off in a sense?

A: Yes. They are not feeling the connection that they have to All That Is that would allow them to know that it is absolutely and always and utterly, every single second, within their capacity to make a choice to be in a state of being that represents absolute joy and they don't need any other reason other than the ones they invent in order to do so. All That Is will never contradict you. In that sense God does not countermand your will. God's will *is* your will. And in that sense, whatever you choose is why you have been given free will and it is the, shall we say, will of God that you have free will and use it to choose what you will. But it will allow you to choose anything. It is that unconditional.

Q: You used the word "God," which on our planet is a pretty loaded word.

A: Yes. Well, that's why we often use "All That Is" as replacement terminology because we understand that the term "God" may have many different interpretations on your planet. But when we choose to use it, it is simply a generalization to make it easy to understand the concept that we are discussing. But often we will use All That Is because that's what the infinite is, the One is. By definition it is all that is. There is no outside to it; there cannot be an outside to it, by definition.

Q: Are a lot of darkness and wounds coming to the surface at this time for humanity to be healed?

A: The idea of your awakening is to bring all the negativity to the surface that might be buried in your unconscious or subconscious selves and deal with it, integrate it. Understand that it's just a part of you. Understand that it needs to be faced. Understand that it needs to be loved. Understand that it needs to be understood. So that you can use it in a positive way. You can learn from it about yourself. Anything that comes to you, any bit of information about yourselves, whether positive or negative, can be applied in a positive way if you so desire. So yes, in this so-called "New Age" or "Age of Awakening" or "age of spiritual awareness" on your planet the whole idea is that you are really at the end of the cycle of limitation that you have imposed on yourselves for thousands of years, and you're awakening to the remembrance that you don't have to do it that way.

> *The whole idea is that you are really at the end of the cycle of limitation that you have imposed on yourselves for thousands of years.*

So that you are bringing all the remnant negativity up, out, bubbling out onto the surface so that you can get it out on the table in plain sight and can make an informed and conscious decision. Is this what we want our world to be, or do we prefer something different? And then, once you make a decision, do something about it instead of hiding it and keeping everything suppressed and secret, which doesn't allow anyone to then deal with the issue, nor to learn from it nor to integrate it.

Q: So could you say, using a bit of a cliché, it's always darkest before the dawn?

A: Yes, exactly so. Darkest before the dawn. We often use what we call a rubber band analogy to describe this mechanism as well. We know you have on your planet this device called a rubber band. And we know that if you pull it back very, very far, the farther back you pull it, when you let it go it will snap that much farther, that much faster onto the other side, into the other direction. Well, the analogy holds for the idea of the exploration of limitation and darkness as well, and answers one of your previous questions as to the degree of darkness and limitation on Earth.

The idea really from the soul's point of view is that the farther into darkness you go, the farther into darkness you explore, the farther back you pull the rubber band onto the dark side, when you finally do decide to let go of that fear and limitation you will snap that much faster and that much farther into the light. So momentum to snap into the light is actually gathered by exploring the darkness as deeply as you can. And then once you decide to integrate all that and not fear it, it will propel you into joy and into passion much more rapidly, and you will have a much faster transition on your planet than you ever had before.

Q: And this is happening now?

A: It is happening now. You are accelerating. By your year of 2012, which has been recognized as a threshold crossing by many intuitive people on your planet, you will have actually in that year crossed the threshold of having slightly more positive energy collectively on your planet than negative. And that will start things accelerating even faster toward the positive so that about two to three decades hence you will find that things have changed so dramatically on your planet it will then be fundamentally positive as opposed to fundamentally negative.

Q: But it will take that long?

A: It still takes a little bit of time because you do after all still experience the idea of a space-time process. But really twenty or thirty years is not long, it's the blink of an eye historically speaking as far as the amount of time you've experienced limitation and negativity on your planet, for thousands and thousands and thousands of years.

Q: What you just described, is it called "ascension"?

A: It is a type of ascension, although again we understand there are many interpretations of that word on your planet. You will still remain in physical reality, but your vibration will be much higher. The idea is that you won't necessarily look that different to each other, but let us say that a person on your planet from three hundred years ago were capable of looking at you today. They would actually see you glowing because your spiritual vibration is so much higher than it was three hundred years ago. But you look around and because you're used to that vibration you don't necessarily see each other glowing with light. But you will continue to glow with more and more light as you increase and enhance and raise your frequency. And in that sense it is a form of ascension.

Eventually humans will ascend into nonphysical dimensional experience, which is what my civilization is in the process of doing now. Going from what might euphemistically be called 4th density reality to 5th density nonphysical reality even as you are going from 3rd density to 4th density. In about one thousand of your years of counting, humans will no longer choose to incarnate on the Earth. Some of the souls may stick around, as you say, to act as nonphysical guides for the next life-form that will appear on Earth and use Earth for its own, shall we say, training ground. But in one thousand years souls will no longer need the human experience on Earth and no more incarnations generally will take place at that time, on your planet, as humans.

Q: Is the Earth a living entity?

A: It is. All things are the product of consciousness and have their own form and expression of consciousness. Because consciousness is what All That Is is. Thus all things take place in and are made out of the consciousness of the one. But consciousness expresses itself in different ways. It may not appear conscious to you, to humans in the way you think of yourselves as conscious, but it is absolutely aware in its own way just as everything on the planet.

Q: Is it true that all souls decide when to depart, die?

A: Fundamentally, yes. Some souls may leave it up to the random events that occur within physical reality so that they do not necessarily lock the window of departure down to a specific time frame as some other souls might. But generally, yes, you choose the time of your birth, you choose the time of your departure. In general. Some will have a window in which that may happen. Give or take a certain number of days, weeks, months, or years depending upon what it is they are choosing to experience.

Q: And do we choose our departure before we're born, or later?

A: It can be both.

Q: We can change it while in flesh?

A: You can if that serves what you are exploring to do so. For most of you it's simply not necessary to change that. But yes, you can.

Q: Is it true that humans have guides or helpers?

A: All humans have guides and helpers, yes. You are all connected to much larger families than you may be aware of.

Q: How many and what type?

A: It will depend. Many of the guides are simply friends that you've experienced other lives with who simply may not be incarnating in the same time frame that you are. Have remained in spirit for that duration to help you from the other side, so to speak. There are some guides that come from what you would call other levels, other dimensions, other realities, that may be serving a purpose in helping you. Not only yours but theirs as well in terms of what they are learning for their own soul's growth.

But most individuals on your planet will have some kind of familial guidance from friends that they have in many ways interacted with before; and generally you will have a primary guide, but you may also have two or three others who are assisting or trading off from time to time depending on how it is they need to help you and what it is they're also learning.

> All *humans have guides and helpers . . . You are all connected to much larger families than you may be aware of.*

Q: What is the best way to connect with them?

A: The easiest way is simply to live your life as passionately as you can so that you're operating on a very high frequency that will then become more receptive to receiving guidance and information from them when and where it is appropriate. The idea is that often a guide will attempt to remain unobtrusive also in giving you the information because the whole point of guiding you is to actually teach you to be your own best guide. So the idea is that many times a guide will use the props that exist in your own physical reality already to get you to pay attention to information that they feel you might need to know or that might serve you.

So for example, synchronicity in life. Those little coincidences that aren't accidental of just winding up at the right place, the right time, overhearing exactly the conversation you needed to hear exactly at the right moment to be able to get that next piece of information you needed at exactly that moment, may have been the work of your guides steering you in a certain direction and not delivering the information directly but knowing the information was available to you in your reality already if they would only nudge you down a certain street at a certain time. That's all they may need to do. So they will often use the synchronicity and the information available in your own reality to get the point across. Sometimes you might actually hear them more strongly and more directly.

You might experience them in your dreams. Very often dream communication is one of the strongest ways that guides will communicate with you, and many of the so-called dreams that you may remember when you wake up may not always have just been the random collection of processing going on in your brain from the day's events but may actually be representative of a communication or conversation you're having with friends and family on other levels.

Q: Have you personally outgrown the need for guides?

A: We have our own guides. There will never be a time when it will be unnecessary to receive help from higher levels, until you actually are the One and then there is no higher level.

Q: And then you sort of start over?

A: So to speak, although remember: All That Is is not subject to time. So yes, you can create the experience of having a new cycle in which to have new experiences. But they can vary, and it takes many forms and it isn't exactly starting over, it's just doing something different. In a new way, from a new perspective. Because remember, everything you experience is the same one moment just from a different point of view.

Because there is only one here and now. Only one existence of All That Is. But the idea is that every single different thing that is experienced as a different thing is simply the same one thing experiencing itself from a different point of view. So that's why we colloquially say that everyone is really just another eye of God. An eye of All That Is, a different perspective All That Is has of itself.

Q: Some people on Earth use Jesus Christ as a guide; what is his true significance?

A: The idea of the Christ consciousness from our perspective is that it represents the collective oversoul of all the spirits on the Earth. It is a very high point of view. But it is analogous to the idea of Buddha nature, Krishna spirit, Christ consciousness. It's all the same idea. The collective spirit, the collective soul of all souls in that sense.

Q: It's so misinterpreted . . .

A: Because of the human's proclivity to be creating experiences of disconnection, and thus creating interpretation from that level. Instead of allowing understanding to exist from the level of the spirit, which is where the information was delivered from. But because physical reality is much denser than the level from which the information came it can find its way into nooks and crannies that can cause distortions in perception.

Q: Will there come a time on Earth when we're not fighting over whose God is best?

A: Yes. As we said, within what you would call the next two to three decades of time you will find that enough has changed on your planet that that will no longer be a practice. It will be understood at that time that all beliefs are true, equally true, because they are all aspects of the same one creation. Thus they are all equally valid.

Q: You said that all lives are being lived simultaneously. So I suppose we have all been killers, and been killed . . .

A: Especially at this point in the cycle, you have pretty much all done it all. That's why you're arriving at the end of the cycle of limitation—because there's really not that much left to explore. You have all done it all. So now you are remembering, you're waking up out of that particular dream because you're at the end of that dream almost.

Q: But we've all explored the darkest corners there are to explore?

A: Almost all of you, yes. There are still in that sense what you might call newcomers on the Earth who haven't necessarily run the gamut of all the different kinds of incarnations that you can have as a human on Earth. But the majority of you, yes, have experienced just about everything you can experience. You have killed and been killed. You have been a benefactor and been benefited. You have been every gender. Every experience. You have been every family member and friend. You have had just about every disease that can be had. You have experienced absolute joy in certain lives. Freedom. Fear. Everything. The whole spectrum. Most of you at this point. Well over 95 percent of you.

Q: What is global warming?

A: It is the effect of a natural cycle on your planet that has been accelerated through artificial means by basis of some of your technologies. So it is a combination of a natural cycle and an artificial acceleration. But it is the cycle that allows for changes to occur on the planet in such a manner as to refresh, reinvigorate, restart a new idea, a new cycle, a new vibration, a new energy. The changes that go on will affect you according to your own beliefs and will, in that sense, be caused by your beliefs, but the acceleration in that sense is coming from many of your own beliefs.

> *All beliefs are true, equally true, because they are all aspects of the same one creation.*

Q: A lot of it is also the Earth cleansing?

A: Yes. It is again a natural cycle, but you have artificially accelerated it and also artificially amplified it.

Q: The part we caused, will it be a hindrance to the Earth?

A: In some senses it is a hindrance. But the Earth is resilient. Understand as you do it has been through many different changes—far more powerful and far more destructive changes than humanity is almost capable of creating. And yet it has recovered. But the idea really is not even so much about the perpetuation of the Earth; it's really about the perpetuation of your own species. So when you talk about the idea of saving the planet what you really mean is "Do you want to save yourselves? Do you want to continue as humanity on the Earth?" Because the Earth will survive.

Q: But we've made that decision haven't we, to continue?

A: On some level you have. Although again, please remember there are an infinite number of parallel realities and all you're actually doing by changing your vibration is shifting yourself to a parallel reality Earth that is already representative of the idea that you will no longer do harmful things. So the old Earth will still be there, and in fact there are many parallel reality Earths that have been utterly destroyed. But you can shift yourself to a parallel reality Earth that is representative of the kind of reality that you prefer to exist in, which obviously requires a change in your behavior to express and exemplify by example that your vibration and desire is representative of something other than what you've been doing.

And that will shift you to the parallel reality Earth that is already representative of the changes. You can experience this as quickly or as slowly as you wish. It is all dependent on how quickly or slowly you shift your frequency. So if you want to see your world change, all you have to do is change yourself sufficiently. And agree with others to do that as well, and then each of you, by agreement, will experience each other in a new Earth, in a new parallel reality that is representative of what you have agreed to experience and you will no longer experience those that had not agreed to experience the same Earth with you. They will still remain in the other parallel reality.

Q: So if someone was convinced by religious belief or whatever that the world was going to end, would they shift to a parallel reality where the world does end?

A: Yes. Absolutely. There are an infinite number of parallel reality experiences. Again, you have absolute free will. That's what it means to have free will in an infinite universe. You can experience anything, even the total destruction of your world. If that is what your belief insists on experiencing, you will experience it absolutely. But again you are still an infinite spirit, you will still go on.

Q: So there is no right and wrong then?

A: Not in that sense. There are positive and negative experiences mechanically speaking. Not so much the subjective good, bad, right, and wrong idea. But you can recognize objectively that positive energy integrates, unifies, amplifies, and that negative energy segregates, separates, is discordant, disharmonious. That's the mechanical definition. So what do you prefer, disharmony and separation, fear and doubt, or harmony, unification, joy, and peace? It's really just a matter of deciding what effects you want and thus which energy you wish to perpetuate in your reality.

Q: We have a saying on Earth: "good grief." Some people enjoy the discord . . .

A: They do. But that's only because they have been taught to believe that nothing else is possible. They may simply be ill-equipped in terms of their tool kit to understand what tools may be available to them to experience something different.

Q: I know we've transmuted many Earth changes; what can we look forward to in the coming years?

A: First of all, remember, all of you, that there is no such thing as a prediction of the future. There are an infinite number of probable future realities, and when someone makes a prediction they are not predicting the future, they are sensing the energy that exists in the present, when the prediction is made. If that energy doesn't change, if it has a great degree of momentum, or inertia, then it is unlikely to shift and it may, as you say, come true. But if it does change, then it renders the prediction obsolete because all the prediction was doing was sensing the energy that existed at the time the prediction was made. And sometimes making the prediction can actually change the energy and render itself obsolete.

So the idea is to understand that no matter what we say we may or may not see coming up as we sense your energy now, it is all changeable. What we sense now is that in your year of 2010 there is still a likelihood that your present location (Los Angeles) may experience a sizeable seismic event. Nevertheless, we understand that your collective energy can render it into a series of smaller seismic events that release the energy harmlessly.

We also recognize that there is still a high degree of potentiality for what you would call a terrorist nuclear incident in the Middle East. Again, it's up to you to change your energy and make it so that that kind of event is unnecessary to experience. However I will tell you this: If that event does come to pass within the next ten years at the outside, if it does come to pass that there is a nuclear strike from a terrorist device in the Middle East, I will tell you that your energy on the planet will change sufficiently from that experience that you will never let it happen again. Ever. But it doesn't have to happen to begin with. You can change that too. All you have to do is remember that you are your governments, and if you begin dialogs of self-empowerment, then you will gain enough momentum on the positive side to diffuse those circumstances before they begin. But that's up to you because it's your planet. We can't really interfere in that context.

The only way we have been able to intervene in the past has been whenever you might have found yourselves on the threshold of actual total nuclear annihilation. Because that will affect not only your world but will interpenetrate different dimensionalities and that we will not allow. So your government and military have been given demonstrations by spacecraft, what you would call UFOs, who have parked themselves over missile silos and deactivated the missiles as a clear sign that we will not let you fire them in an all-out global nuclear war. But we cannot prevent isolated events. But you can.

> *There are an infinite number of probable future realities, and when someone makes a prediction they are not predicting the future, they are sensing the energy that exists in the present.*

Q: Why is the government keeping the UFOs a secret?

A: For a variety of reasons. Again a lot of it has to do with fear, disconnection, belief that the society will panic, belief that your society will collapse, and we have to respect that because you have put people in charge who are saying that's what will happen so we have to keep this a secret, then you are the ones responsible for allowing that to continue. But if you wish there to be disclosure, then you can become active in all the ways that would allow yourselves to know you are ready for more information and thus allow your representatives to deliver more information. Again, that's in your hands.

Q: What if we just decide on an individual basis?

A: Sometimes you can and sometimes you have; however many of the people who think they are ready for contact are not. We have discovered that because your physical consciousnesses exist in such a compartmentalized fashion where you've actually hidden portions of yourselves from yourselves, in your subconscious minds, things that you are afraid to look at, we understand that should you come into contact with a being that represents a much more integrated energy, a higher frequency of energy, that energy might overwhelm the compartmentalized energy of your personality and might force those compartments to break down, dissolve, and might force you to face things you're not ready to face in yourself. And thus the potential to cause psychic shock within you is still great.

So we do not force that. We simply allow each individual to really show when they are ready for that kind of contact. And when they are ready, it will occur. Now I will tell you something else. Many contacts have already occurred in a slightly altered state of dimensionality to allow for the psychic shock to be buffered. But you do not remember those contacts because they take place in a shifted reality. But many of you have had actual contact but you are made to not remember so it does not intervene or interfere with your own process of integration.

Q: Does that also happen in the sleep state?

A: It does, but I'm actually talking about actual contact, physical contact but in a slightly altered dimension of reality.

Q: So there will come a time within about thirty years when our space brothers will be walking among us?

A: Yes. It will be sparse at first. To allow you to get used to the idea. But eventually, somewhere around your year of 2033 to 2037, you will as a planet be given honorary beginning membership in the "Alliance of Worlds." And you will begin your true relationship with us. That's how we read the energy now.

Q: What is a lightworker?

A: An individual who simply remembers that they are connected to spirit and can consciously allow higher vibratory energies to be brought or channeled through the body for positive effects. For positive applications on the Earth. Many children being born on your planet now are automatic, natural lightworkers because they are really not forgetting as much of who they are as spirits. Not forgetting the connection, not forgetting what they have access to. And they will exemplify this on your planet more and more every day as they grow.

Q: Aren't most children like that?

A: In some senses, but now more than ever. Many of the children that have been born on your planet within the last fifteen years are not only a new generation—they are literally genetically a new species, and actually have greater genetic capacity to access higher levels of energy. They are better antennas, better receivers physiologically, so to speak. So yes, children have always generally had that capacity and they get learned out of it, shall we say? Taught out of it, generally by the age of three. Definitely by the age of seven in your reality. But now not so much anymore. They are coming through with what you would call core fortification, and having this core of their being fortified by certain energetic frequencies, they are less prone to absorb the telepathic onslaught of negative belief systems from the rest of society. They simply won't participate in those beliefs.

Q: Will there come a time when we are so empowered that we won't seek or need channeled material anymore?

A: This format will cease to exist as you become more capable of accessing your own information, yes. We are in a job to put ourselves out of a job by teaching you that you have all the same capacity that we do and that you can access whatever you need when you need it. So we are here to remind you that you don't need us, yes. But we are happy to be your friends and share with you as equals.

Q: How much do we decide before we're born?

A: It depends on the kind of life that you have chosen to live. There are souls that have determined just about every single moment, but that doesn't happen so much anymore. Generally speaking, just the generalities are decided. To whom you will be born. Generally when you will be born. Generally when you will die. Generally what themes you will explore. Generally with whom you will form friendships. Generally where you will exist on the planet or where you will travel to. Those kinds of things are generally chosen by most spirits. Anything more concrete than that is relatively rare nowadays unless it serves some particular purpose of example.

Q: Are we in the process of becoming human angels or is that a misnomer?

A: We understand the connotation that you are simply raising your frequency, and that can be a representation of that idea of balancing the idea within you of polarity so that you express only the positive side. If that is what you wish to call becoming human angels, so be it. But it is simply the idea of the upliftment of your frequency so you can express more of yourself more fully in a positive way in your reality.

Q: As we're becoming more light-filled, where does the dark go?

A: It doesn't go anywhere, it simply becomes more balanced. The idea, remember, is that growth and ascension are the product of integration of all that you are, not the exclusion of anything. It is the allowance that everything is valid.

The balancing of everything is valid so that you can then simply choose what you wish to express without discounting what you don't prefer to express. It is the incorporation of everything, that's why the more evolved you become, you actually become more aware of more dark because you're willing to integrate it and balance it all within you.

Remember that All That Is, the One, is aware of all the light and all the dark that it contains. So as you become more aware of the light, you'll become more aware of the dark. And by allowing that to be a choice that's equally valid to the light, you are then not empowering one side or the other over the other and are simply free to choose whatever you wish.

Q: A key to balance must be that you have to accept and even love the dark parts of yourself?

A: Yes, of course. Allowance, as we said. Acceptance, as we said. Because it is a valid choice.

> *Growth and ascension are the product of integration of all that you are, not the exclusion of anything.*

Q: So many people shut off the dark parts and try to bury them.

A: There is no place to bury them. Anything you push against will always resist because there is nowhere to push anything away to. That's how it amplifies. When you try to judge something as invalid, you are attempting to push it where there is no place to push it to, and it will recoil that much more strongly because you're giving it energy just in the same way you build up the energy of a spring when you collapse it. Because there's nowhere for it to go, it will push against the wall, and when you give it enough energy, it will spring back tenfold and you won't be able to resist it. So the idea is to simply allow it to be a relaxed spring with no built-up energy. Then you can simply choose what spring you prefer.

Q: So the saying "What you resist persists" is true?

A: Yes, and I've just explained mechanically why. Because there's nowhere to get rid of anything to, there's no outside.

Q: Why would a soul choose to be born in a place like, say, Darfur? Why would they want that experience?

A: There again may be as many reasons as there are souls. Look at the idea of individuals who are born into dire circumstances. Can you imagine a positive effect that might come from that? Here's an example, it's been going on on your planet a long time. How do you know that it will only take one more person choosing to be born in that circumstance that will then inspire some other people somewhere else to make sure that that circumstance never happens on Earth? A soul might then choose to say it's worth it. If being born in that circumstance will actually inspire that circumstance to never happen again, it's worth me experiencing that. And from the soul's point of view it will be worth it. So it takes examining of every specific case as to what it is that soul may be getting out of having chosen that experience, because it may be for a variety of reasons.

Often when someone chooses a life such as what you call severe handicapped situations, it isn't even so much that they're choosing it for their own experience. They may be choosing it because of what it will solicit from those around them that are involved with them, like friends or family and how they respond to the situation. It may be teaching them a lesson even more than something the soul that's doing it needs to get out of it. It may simply be doing that out of love for the family in terms of what the family will learn by dealing with a person in that situation. There are as many reasons as there are people.

Q: Using that logic, then Hitler sort of did a service to humanity?

A: From that logic, yes. Again, understand that there is a difference between condoning the idea of perpetrating those kinds of acts and understanding how you can use them in a positive way. Because it is that person's duty to themselves and responsibility to everyone else to not have to succumb to that level of fear so that they must perpetrate those kinds of acts of atrocity upon other people. That's their duty, and he may simply have not achieved that duty. Nevertheless the fact that such a being existed in your reality is part and parcel a reflection of what your reality allows, and thus it is a service to you to show you this is what you support. Is this what you want to continue to support or do you want to change this in the future? So it can be used as a service in that way. So yes, on the soul level it may be looked at as a service even though on the human level it may only be seen as an atrocity.

Q: What happens after a soul passes on?

A: Primarily whatever the being believed would happen. That's what it first experiences generally. Whatever the strongest belief is or possibility is, is generally what the spirit will immediately experience. But there will be those who are there to guide, to help, to open its eyes, so to speak. To help it remember that it is really now in a more natural state. The idea for most individuals when they pass on into spirit is that it's like a physical person waking up from a dream. Just as you wake up from a dream during the night and say "Oh, well that's just fading away, that wasn't real," so too a soul may find itself, a spirit may find itself suddenly in spirit going "Oh, this is who I really am, that was just a dream."

But it will learn from it, add that experience to itself. But again, it depends on the degree of belief systems that surround the death as to what the spirit takes with it as its capability of remembering or recognizing that in fact it has crossed over. Because some spirits do not. It's rare, but some spirits do not know they are dead because of the degree of belief systems they may have harbored as a physical personality. But it's rare. Most will recognize that something has changed and most will get the help they need to recognize exactly what it is that has changed. And then most will remember, in fact, that this is who they are. They will know who they are as a spirit, they will know why they chose that life, and they will get to experience all the ramifications and consequences of all the acts they undertook in that life so they can use that for their own growth.

Q: So they would in a sense go through the pain again?

A: It isn't experienced quite the same way. But they will go through all the experiences and all the consequences of the experiences of anyone else they may have impacted. Because you see in spirit there is no separation between you and others as there is in a space-time continuum. So anything you do that affects another, you will experience the effect from that person's point of view in spirit.

Q: Will it all be experienced in a split second?

A: From our perspective in physical reality, yes. It would appear to be a split second. From the spirit's point of view it may be experienced in a variety of ways. But generally speaking it will be understood in a different way, it will be experienced in a different way. It will not be experienced in the same way a human ego would experience the concept of pain or anxiety, but the soul, the spirit, will experience the idea of the positive and negative consequences in a way that will allow it to assess itself and balance itself as it wishes to.

Q: If somebody had a firm belief in hell would they experience hell?

A: At first, but you see, the experience might be so overwhelming that they would suddenly find themselves wishing that they were not there and instantly of course they would not be there. Because, again, there is no time lag in spirit. Whatever it is you believe or wish, at that moment, most strongly, will instantaneously manifest without any time differential. So as soon as they find themselves in the burning in the flames of hell experience, they may suddenly say I can't take this and suddenly be out of it. Unless of course they are extremely insistent on masochism.

Q: Life has been described as a grand game; do you subscribe to that?

A: Well yes, depends on what kind of spin, as you say, you put on the word "game." It's not that it does not in that sense contain a serious aspect. But yes, it is your call, it is your game, it is your creation, it is your experience. It's up to you. As I said, life is fundamentally meaningless so that you are given the opportunity to give it whatever meaning you decide it shall have in any experience. So it's your call, it's your game. But we do not wish to use the word game to make it seem that it's frivolous. Because it isn't. It is profound.

≡

Ninety minutes had melted away. I knew Darryl generally didn't like to channel for more than two hours at a time because it can by physically draining for him, so I reluctantly shifted into wrap-up mode. Did Bashar have any wise words with which to leave us?

"To be succinct, I would just say: 'Live your dreams . . . instead of dreaming about living.'" This could smack of bumper sticker reductivism, or perhaps something an aunt might needlepoint on a throw pillow. But with all that had come before, it really struck a chord with me, seemed like the ideal capper.

"And so we thank you for the gift of sharing," Bashar concluded, "because you allow us the gift of seeing through all of you that many more ways that creation has of expressing itself, and it expands our understanding of All That Is. So we simply extend our unconditional love, our deep appreciation and heartfelt thanks for the co-creation of this transmission. And we bid you a fond and *exciting* 'good day.'"

A whoosh of air escaped Darryl's lungs, and his entire upper body convulsed. A few seconds later he was rubbing his eyes, looking somewhat wrung out, and asking in a quiet voice, "How did it go?"

"Amazing," was about all I could muster. "Thank you so much."

I was feeling a strange combination of relaxation and exhaustion, as if I'd just been immersed for two hours in a turbo Jacuzzi.

When I asked Darryl if he remembered any of the encounter—questions I'd asked, anything—he said no. "I'm a deep-trance channel, so my consciousness literally goes away and his takes over. It's like I slide over in the seat and let Bashar drive. Some light-trance channelers remember all or some of what goes on, but not me."

As Matt packed equipment, I couldn't help but think

that he looked a bit shaken. Later, he revealed that the session got his attention like a roundhouse kick to the solar plexus.

"The energy in the room was so intense that a few times I found myself almost shaking and barely able to hold up the camera," he told me. "I'm still processing it all. The information that came through was incredible, and Bashar was like a force of nature."

Matt had of course heard of channeling before this, but wasn't as well-versed in the subject as I was, and he'd never seen it in person. "I was a little leery about the entire project," he admitted. "I had a few nights where I questioned what I was getting myself into. But this has pretty much blown me away. I was struck by how smooth and detailed Bashar's answers were on every single subject. No hemming or hawing, no 'ers' or 'ahs,' no hesitation at all. It was nothing short of incredible. I mean, either he's the greatest actor on Earth or this is really happening. I am really excited to find out where this journey takes us."

So was I.

Two

Wendy Kennedy Channeling the Pleiadian Collective

M att and I only spoke once in the next week, about a couple of technical issues. We reconnoitered at the modest Santa Monica apartment of channeler Wendy Kennedy. I'd never met her, but the information on her website, *higherfrequencies.net*, had spoken to me in a deep way. I'd called her only a couple weeks before and asked if she wanted to participate in the film.

Wendy said she'd have to think about it. She called back a few days later and said that the "Pleiadian Collective," a group of 2,500 highly evolved beings she channels from the "ninth dimension" who speak as one, was delighted with the invitation. She was in.

As Matt set up equipment, I was able to chat with Wendy and was impressed with her poise and calm, centered energy. She was thirty-nine at the time, her lineless porcelain face framed by black shoulder-length locks. For some reason, I'd expected these channelers to be somewhat, well, goofier in person; maybe blowing sacred smoke about the room, wearing flowing robes, or stroking a crystal skull. But these first two were as normal as anyone you'd meet in the grocery store line. As Matt put it, "I guess I was expecting these people to be closer to characters from *The Lord of the Rings* or something, but they're just regular people like the rest of us."

A refugee from the business world, Wendy began her channeling journey when she started having visions— sort of like "lucid waking dreams," she explained. "I didn't really know what was going on. I even had a few moments where I thought maybe I was going a little crazy.

"But I trusted my inner guidance, which kept nudging me to look into channeling, something I really knew nothing about and had no interest in at that point."

So she kept doing research, read books on the subject, and started doing the exercises the books recommended. "Then about a year after this, I had my first real breakthrough with automatic writing, which is where you sit down, clear your mind, and let this other energy or spirit or however you want to term it come through. So I did automatic writing for two years, just on my own, not daily, certainly not seeing clients or offering advice or anything like that."

The writing slowly morphed into verbal channeling, and now Wendy has clients all over the globe. "I now know this is why I came to Earth, to do this work," she said. "It's just so very fulfilling to help people, and the Pleiadians now seem like my very best friends and allies."

Matt was ready to get rolling, so Wendy took her seat under the lights and, as with Darryl Anka, I first asked her about her own life before getting into the channeling proper.

I was curious about whether she told family and friends early on about her burgeoning curious avocation. "I was very lucky," she said with a smile. "I have a lot of support. My friends were very accepting. And it's one thing I've always been really open about. I didn't really hide it, even from employers, you know. And, I've always felt that it was really important for me to be honest about that, because I saw how it impacted people."

I asked Wendy to go into a bit more detail, and this time on camera, about how it all started for her.

"About fifteen years ago, I started having visions, and I didn't know what they were," she said, "so I started doing some research on past lives, and I came across channeling. And it was the early '90s and I didn't know anything about it. I didn't know anybody who did it. I just knew it was something I was supposed to be doing. So I found a couple books and did some of the exercises and had really visceral responses, but nothing really happened. I was trying to channel verbally, and my limbs would tingle and my eyes would water. So I would try it periodically and kind of put it aside and come back to it, and took a meditation class and did some other things and did some work on myself. And about a year after I started trying, I sat down one day and just knew I was supposed to have a pencil and paper and started to do automatic writing. And it's kinda developed over the years."

Wendy believes she is not particularly special or gifted, and that everyone actually channels whether they call it that or not.

"We all have the ability to channel," she said. "I define channeling as bringing in energy and translating it into a recognizable form: speaking, dancing, writing, drawing, or any other creative expression. The source of the energy can be from our higher self, our guides, people we loved on Earth now departed, or from other dimensions and realities. It's really just a matter of choosing a particular frequency, like you would a radio station, and turning up the volume."

But why her—why would she have this unique calling? "Oh, it was definitely something I set up and agreed to do before I incarnated in this body," she said matter-of-factly. "I've done similar work in other lifetimes and have been persecuted, even killed, for doing it. But this lifetime is very different. It really is the Great Shift or whatever you want to term it. People are ready to awaken and that's why the Pleiadians are connecting, to help us do just that. But they can tell you more about that," she concluded with a wry smile.

Moments later, Wendy had closed her eyes and was taking deep breaths. But there were none of the extreme facial tics and comparative histrionics that Anka had shown. About ten seconds passed, a smile eased onto her face, and an altered voice emerged. It was a bit higher pitched than Wendy's own, and the accent reminded me of an English governess in an old movie, a bit clipped but brimming with positive energy.

After a warm greeting of "Yes, hello dear, we are very pleased to be with you today," the Collective explained the reason for the shift in Wendy's voice.

≡

Many people will ask, "why do they sound British? Why do they sound this way or that way?" It is because we are working with you with a tonal language. It's almost as if you're having healing. You are getting many, many levels of information. And as we tell you that it is a nice day, we are depositing an energetic packet within your field that tells you "it is 70 degrees, there's a light breeze, the roses are very fragrant." There's a lot more information. So those who are watching the movie or reading these words are also going to receive this downloaded information. What would you like to know about first?

> *We all have the ability to channel . . . It's really just a matter of choosing a particular frequency . . . and turning up the volume.*

≡

I noticed immediately that the Pleiadian energy was much different than the crisp gusts Bashar emitted. This was more like having a conversation with a loving aunt while sitting in an easy chair and eating a hot fudge sundae: very comfortable and relaxing.

≡

Q: Could you please tell us why you are coming through Wendy at this time on Earth?

A: Part of it is that it is our agreement, it is part of our contract . . . and she is actually part of the collective. Which is a question that she has not asked herself. So that is a brand-new tidbit for her. And we're coming through at this time because we are not happy with the way that things exist currently in our reality. We are from what you would perceive to be the future, and we have come back to our past so that we may learn and so that we may assist the planet because what's going on now is going to impact the entire universe. And we really want to see things change.

There was the potential for the entire game to be destroyed. That's something that's not talked about because we don't want you to focus on it. But there was the potential the way things were going energetically for some very unfortunate events to occur that would create a lot of destruction and we really didn't want to walk down that path. So we're here to help change that.

Q: Has some of that already been changed?

A: Yes, quite a bit of it actually. And you have outdone yourselves in a sense. This has never been done before, where a planet has transited with conscious beings on it. All of the best of the best got to come down to the game this go-round. You're always looking to the higher frequencies, you're looking to the celestial realms as if there is some hierarchy where there are beings who have more information than you have, who have more answers than you have. And what we tell you is that you are the ones who have all of the answers. You are the ones who are down here writing the books, writing the lessons on how it's all done. So we're all learning from you.

Q: That seems odd. I mean, if we're such masters, then why is there so much unhappiness and even despair on Earth and so many people who just don't realize they are masters?

A: That's part of duality. You can't have one without the other, and now you are coming to a point where you're bringing in so much light you've got that polarity. You've got that other extreme and you cannot have one without the other. You can't have all that information and light coming in without that darkness when you're still in duality in the third dimension, because when you're looking at dimensions within this particular system within the universe duality exists throughout the dimensions. But the higher the dimension you go into, duality is not as extreme as it is. The lower in frequency you go, the more intense duality becomes. That's why you have so many people going through so much pain. And it also is, believe it or not, serving a purpose.

> *Until you understand that you're holographic in nature—what happens to the microcosm happens to the macrocosm—you will never be fully able to heal yourselves.*

From the higher perspective, you know, pain serves its purpose. It is a catalyst for change because if you were happy and content all the time you probably wouldn't move, would you? No. So it serves as a catalyst, and we will tell you pain is perception, nothing more. If you were to tell one person that you think they have a large nose, they're going to look at you strangely and think, "alright, that was an odd statement." And if you were to say it to another who was self-conscious, they would be devastated. It's all in perception and what you create internally in the emotional field. Some people are creating these drastic events in order to wake up, in order to get their own attention.

When you get to a level where there are drastic events, it is occurring because you have not been paying attention before that. You have been suppressing the emotional experience. And it comes right back around in a more intensified form to get your attention. Because this beautiful reality that you've created for yourself is displaying what's going on on an emotional level for you.

And as a collective the planet is reflecting what's going on emotionally, and the planet is not in a very good shape right now. You have polluted your oceans. You have devastated some of your lands and that is also going on on an internal level. Until you understand that you're holographic in nature—what happens to the microcosm happens to the macrocosm—you will never be fully able to heal yourselves.

Q: So reducing it to shorthand, once we heal ourselves we'll heal the planet?

A: Yes, that's exactly it. Enough of you are beginning to see that and beginning to understand that and what's happening is you are creating a new version of the planet.

Q: Is there a timetable for this, or do we just do it as we do it?

A: There is an acceleration, and you're feeling it. This push, things speeding up, that there aren't as many hours in the day, as it were. And that's very true. There aren't as many hours in the day because time is compressing. Because as you get higher in frequency and closer to the fourth dimension, time ceases to exist. That's where you get, in your records, the end times. Because time will cease to exist in the same fashion in the other dimensions.

Q: So as we heal ourselves does your world also change?

A: Yes, it does. This gets into time and altering time, so we will try to explain it, but try not to process it all through your head; try to work with your heart, because you'll go in circles in your head. There are multiple timelines, multiple realities. And as you are changing one, it changes other probable realities. Because they all exist beside each other. We have chosen to stand in one that is very out of balance. Just like you, we don't like to be bored, we like challenges . . . so here we are. We want to change things, and as you change, we are learning lessons. We are learning for instance about compassion, integrating duality.

There are some fine lessons being learned down here. We're learning from you what that means, because you are so immersed in dark energy and you're coming out of such a very dark place that you're learning some tremendous lessons in the process. But it's very hard for you to see that because you're standing in the middle of it. That's why we say you really are the masters, you just can't see because you're in the middle of it.

Q: Why have we decided to keep ourselves in darkness and duality for so long?

A: In the grand scheme it's but a blink of the eye. There are many levels and layers regarding this. There have been humans who have been in other star systems. There are other species that are not humanoid that they have incarnated with. One of the universal laws is that you're holographic in nature, and that translates as, "as above, so below." So if you think of the United States as a melting pot, all the strife that you go through as a country, with your prejudices, that's happening out in the galaxy. It's not all light and airy. There's a lot of conflict out there as well, and that's just part of the game.

Q: Is this the only game to play, the light and dark game with conflict and war, or is there another game we'll find more appealing as we progress?

A: There are lots of different versions of the game. It depends on the things you want to focus on. Perhaps it is learning how to restructure material so that you can create a star or a planet. There are beings that go to work on that. But even within that you've got systems of duality, there are basic rules to the universe and how it works. So in this universe it's duality. In other universes it can be singularity or you can have multiples. You have trinary systems. It gets very difficult for us to explain it because you're all wanting to process it through your brain and you're so immersed in duality that it just seems completely foreign.

Q: You're a collective of 2,500 beings; how do you all agree on something?

A: We don't always agree 100 percent. But what we are capable of doing is to understand and connect with another to really grasp their viewpoint and see where their perspective is coming from. So it's about being empathic in a sense. We don't always agree but the majority does rule. And you've got a lot of beings who are coming in, you'll hear about a lot of councils and federations. It is a step toward a collective consciousness, but it is still working within physicality. We're at a higher level as it were; many of us have been through the physical process but where we are energetically able to connect. You're always connected to a collective because you're always connected to source and source is the entire collective.

Q: How would you say humanity is doing generally with the ascension process?

A: Very well. It's not easy and we understand that. For the most part you've done better than most of us had expected. Your 9/11 created a whole new level. There was the potential for that event to create a lot of anger, a lot of distrust, a lot of retaliation, and a lot of lower responses, but many of you responded instead with compassion. And that altered your timeline dramatically.

Q: And yet our leaders still took us to war.

A: Yes, well there's a whole other game being played there, dear. There are other beings who are manipulating and controlling events on the planet. They have a vested interest in it as well, and we're talking about the Annunaki. While they are not human in the sense that they have incarnated to Earth, they are humanoid. They are not reptilian. Many of the reptilians that you hear about, those are Pleiadians. There are reptilians from other star systems as well but they are the front men. They are being projected to generate fear. Because you have been cocooned, isolated. Your history has been rewritten so that you don't remember who and what you truly are so that you can be utilized. If you're being presented with this notion that someone is not human, that's frightening to you because you think you are all that exists.

Q: How do the Annunaki control the leaders?

A: Part of it is through genetic lines. That's because there is genetic memory of being connected and being controlled and being manipulated. Not everyone is being controlled, per se, but they are so deeply entrenched in this game, consumption and power, that is the track they are on. So they may not know that they're being played, as it were. But there are beings that are connected with these extraterrestrials, if you will, who know the true history. And they are assisting. But they are not the ones who are out at the front.

Q: Are the Annunaki on their way out on Earth?

A: There are multiple versions of Earth that are going to begin to separate. They are all existing right now one on top of another, and they're all different bands of frequency. As you get closer to 2012, those bands and frequencies are going to become more distinct and where you're vibrating at is going to determine which version you're standing on.

That's why you have those who will go into the fourth dimension and those who will go into the third dimensional version as far as they can. It's really about ranges of frequency, and when you're talking about the Annunaki, you're talking about "which band are they standing in?" But we will tell you that it is very important that the Annunaki go through this ascension process with you, because they are playing the role of the dark. You need someone to play that role and they have donned it, and they have been in the dark for so long.

> *There are multiple versions of Earth that are going to begin to separate . . . all existing right now one on top of another, and they're all different bands of frequency.*

Think about it this way. Think of how you would feel if you had never felt love, or that you felt love but it was so long ago you really can't remember it. That's rather tragic, and that's where they're at. So rather than fear them or feel anger with them, our goal is not to instill fear. It's to understand their place. And it's finding this place of compassion like a child. They too need to be brought back into love and know what love is, and that's part of why they are involved with this ascension process. Because they too are coming to the end of a cycle. They have donned this role, this heavy role, and they too need to clear that energy.

Q: Are they consciously aware of this?

A: Not at all. They are so trapped in the lower frequencies. This is why they are using the planet and its natural resources and why they generate so much fear. You have the capability to tap into the frequency of love. You have the ability to open up your energetic field to source energy. They, however, are so immersed in fear and anger and retribution and power and control that they can't access that feeling of love. So what they do is amass all this lower frequency energy and it allows them to open up dimensional portals.

Q: And their "power" essentially comes from us giving it to them?

A: Yes. That's why they create this game to keep you in fear. That's one level of it. They're feeding off the fear. Their other game is keeping you from remembering who and what you truly are so you don't take your toys and go play in another sandbox.

Q: But in spite of that we are remembering.

A: Yes, and they are very nervous because this is all they know. So they are making an effort to prevent things from changing. We're not saying this is all Annunaki—that would be like lumping all Earthlings together in how they feel about things. It is this one particular group that has decided that they are resisting change.

Q: Are we influenced by them when we feel greed or negative energy, or is that our doing?

A: Both. You're a willing participant, so you're playing the game. They started that game going, so you're playing their game. But you can unplug from that and you can create your own version of the game.

Q: Do you have practical advice for how people can raise their frequency and make this all more graceful and easy?

A: We always like the question "what am I here to do? What is my job?" And we'll tell you: It's just to live life. As you're wanting to clear and ascend, it's really just dealing with your life and taking a look at what you are creating, what is in front of you. As we've said before, this physical reality is reflecting absolutely everything that you need to know, so are you paying attention? Or are your eyes closed? Working on yourself is the greatest gift that you can give to humanity.

And that sounds so self-centered and so negative, but that's how you've been conditioned. If you understand that you're holographic in nature and you can clear it in yourself, then it makes it much easier for others to clear.

> Working on yourself is the greatest gift that you can give to humanity.

There's a lot of power in that. So if you want to keep someone from accessing their own power and helping to heal the planet or helping to heal mass consciousness, you're going to tell them that it's very selfish for them to look inside.

So what can you do for yourself? Look at your issues. Where are your buttons being pushed? Where do you feel fear? Where do you feel that you shrink away? And those are the places that you need to look at. We will tell you that we find there are several healing modalities that are far more powerful, and we will also say that your healing modalities are going to start changing very radically. For a while now you've had your reiki and your sekhem and qigong and your general hands-on healing. And it's wonderful. It was very good for the masses, a very gentle way to start to bring things up.

But we're going to tell you it's time to up the game. You're running out of time. We don't want to say that with you thinking you're feeling pressured, but things are going to start to accelerate. You're going to be able to move through things very quickly. Whereas before it may have taken you several years, it's going to take you several days or several hours. You're going to have a lot of your core issues come up to the surface. It's not that something's wrong or that you're doing something wrong—it's part of the clearing process so you can move into the higher frequencies without this baggage from the third dimension. And you want to deal with it now because it's going to be far more intense for you to deal with it later, because it's immediately manifest and it's far more of an intense manifestation.

So as you move into this next cycle, it is going to be about fifty years' worth of growth in an approximate eight-month period. And if you think that is intense, the one coming after that is going to be several lifetimes worth of growth in a six-month period. You wonder how in the world will we all be able to ascend; it seems like we're falling so far behind, but we are telling you that you are getting support and time is going to accelerate, you're going to move through things very, very quickly.

Q: What are some of these healing modalities?

A: Working with tone and sound is one of the most potent, the most powerful. And there are different reasons for that. One is that with the human voice there is also an emotional carrier wave that goes along with it. If the healer is in a space of unconditional love, that emotional carrier wave goes right along with it. So when you work with tone and sound and you work with harmonics, what happens is that note begins to vibrate up mathematically.

And as you get higher, you start to move into other dimensions, and it will clear out through multiple dimensions. That's why tone and sound and harmonics are so incredibly powerful: because they're working through multiple dimensions. And the emotional range that accompanies this body goes up to the sixth dimension. So you're not only clearing out the physical; you're also working with the emotional body, the one that you're taking with you. When you incorporate instruments, it's like having another layer of filter on there, it's something else that the energy has to transmit through in order to get to you. While it's possible, and a lot of energy and positive things can occur through that, it's not as potent.

The other is breath work, working with your breath. Because there are different kinds of breathing. Just as you blow on a fire, there are different ways of breathing on a fire to achieve different results. Do you want to get the flame very high and very hot, or what do you want the flame to do? The breath works energetically and physically. It stokes your energetic field, allowing you to bring issues up to the surface so they can be released. The emotional body creates the physical template.

All illness starts in the emotional field, without exception. If it's a genetic mutation, that starts in the emotional field, and it is something that has been so generously left behind by one of your ancestors. They had a big emotional issue, a block, and it altered the genetic material and that got passed down to the genetic line. That can also be altered. If you can clear it out of your field, it can clear it out of the genetic line. You clear out emotionally; the physical template then responds to the change in the emotional one. So if there are toxins locked in cells because of that block in the energetic field, those are then released and the oxygen helps to move those particles through the body.

> All *illness starts in the emotional field, without exception.*

Q: And there'll be new modalities as well?

A: Yes. As some of you begin to understand how to move multidimensionally, you can come back and work multidimensionally through the energetic bodies. As you are working and clearing things out of your body, you are clearing through not only this lifetime but also other lifetimes. Every experience of those other aspects of yourself is reflected in your energetic field. You are the walking library. That entire life is deposited in your energetic field. So all those issues that that other lifetime didn't want to deal with or suppressed are showing up in your auric field.

What happens is that sometimes you have issues in your life that are in resonance with that issue from another lifetime. Perhaps it's the issue of self-love. As you come into that issue, the two vibrate together and intensify, and sometimes you will have past life memories. They're coming up to get your attention because something in your life is in resonance with that and it's beginning to vibrate. So you can see it to clear it. This go-round you are clearing things out on a personal level, and then you start to clear out all of that other stuff, all those other blockages from other lifetimes and from your genetic line. Fair or not, you have chosen this one to be the lifetime that gets to process all the other unfinished business. This is the conscious state that is going to take this body into the fourth dimension, and you want a clean house. So it is important.

Many of you ask "what role do past lives play?" and we will tell you that they play a very big one. They're not really past, they're concurrent. As you are both working on things, you are clearing things out energetically. Through both emotional bodies. That's enough to make your head spin. Many of you who have been awake for a while are starting to clear out these other lifetimes, you're starting to have more of these memories because you're getting to those deeper levels of your emotional field that really need to be cleared. The final stages as it were. So that was a very long answer to your question.

Q: Is it true that in these past or concurrent lives, we've really done it all? We've all been killers, monks, women, men?

A: Yes. There are many who would like to think they've been nothing but the light, but we'll say: One, how boring is that? And two, you've been both. For those of you who are extremely light, guess what? You've had extremely dark lifetimes. You've probably done some extremely dastardly deeds. So that's difficult. Part of your "new age movement" wants to be all light and all happy, and we'll tell you, that is not what this lifetime is about. Because there are prejudices there. And the idea here is that you release all of that prejudice, all of that judgment against the dark. Because you cannot have one without the other.

That's a different mind-set there. There are some who want to step into that space and say "ooh, I'm nothing but light, I haven't had any dark lifetimes." And we will tell you, it is precisely the opposite. Because usually it's not until you have mastered the dark or some aspect of the dark that you are given abilities to work in the light as well.

Q: A lot of people may not have heard of channeling and might say that this type of communication is impossible. What would you say to them?

A: We would say it's very much like your radio stations. It is all about energy, it is all about frequency. Nothing more, nothing less. And you are the receiver, you are tuning in to it. Just as your eyes are able to interpret frequency waves and send them to the brain, it is no different with emotions. And that is what we are sending you. Emotions, information on a carrier wave, on a frequency. But you have to find the station, and you have to turn the volume up. Right now most of you have the volume turned down. Each and every one of you has the ability to channel. You do it every day, you just don't realize that you're doing it. You work with your oversoul, you work with your higher consciousness, you work with your guides, you work with your dearly departed. Just as your eyes cannot see ultraviolet rays, that you cannot perceive them doesn't mean they don't exist. These frequencies are there, you may just not be aware. You're not interpreting the signal.

So how does one interpret a signal? One, it's clearing the static on the line. In other words, clearing out the static in your body. Clearing out some of the lower frequencies that prohibit you from hearing, and that's why more and more channels are coming forth—because they are clearing out their energetic fields. People are raising their frequencies, and it's making it much easier to connect with the other side. If you're looking at someone who is psychic, they are tapping into Akashic records and probable realities. That's one station. The dearly departed, that's another station. Your angels and guides, that's another. And here we are, your extraterrestrials, at the other end.

There is a smorgasbord of stations to listen to, things to try, lots of beings who want to communicate. Some of them are your "families," your star families who are working with a good number of you at night. When you go through a long sleep and you're tired when you wake up, it's because you've been busy working. Out of your body, working to get information. And some of you are reporting back, "this is what it's like on Earth." You may have been at a podium addressing the masses on other planets. You're checking in and telling everyone what's going on. Because, as you know, not everyone got to come.

Q: How would one effectively communicate with a dead relative?

A: Well first, we would say you have to surround yourself and protect yourself with beautiful white light, and relax. The greatest issue is the anxiety that comes up—there are usually memories of pain and loss and disconnection that keep you from connecting. If you can relax and envision this eternal connection that you have with other beings, it puts you at ease and opens you up to higher frequencies. It makes it much easier for you then to communicate, to hear, because you're removing the static on the line. So if you can clear out your own energetic field by feeling unconditional love, surround yourself with peace, white light, love, ask for assistance from the beings of the highest light and love, all others bind from you, be very clear about that. And then, imagine that connection. Hear that connection.

You have not been conditioned to remember what this connection is like, you've forgotten what it's like, it may seem very much like your imagination as you begin. But then, we always say to you, "what is your imagination anyway?" That's another one that will make your head spin. While it may seem like your imagination to begin with, it is that initial connection. You will begin to turn that volume up, and you will begin to sense within your own body subtle differences, that it is not just you, it is not just your "imagination." You will begin to get the confirmation. Your guides and beings on the other side are your biggest support group. They want you to succeed, so they are going to try over and over again to make sure you get the information.

Q: How many guides does a person generally have?

A: It really depends upon the soul, but if you are talking about the guides that are with you throughout multiple lifetimes: Because you are in a system of duality you have set up for yourselves, you've got two. Two main guides, and then you are working with others that you've made contracts with, who we consider to be guides as well.

Q: I guess communicating with them would be similar to communicating with a deceased relative?

A: It is precisely the same. You're just envisioning and being clear about who you want to connect with. One of the biggest things that prohibits people from connecting is *asking*. You've all forgotten how to ask for what you want. That's a big one. We don't always give information, you've got to ask. Because when you ask you are consciously seeking, you are telling the universe, "this is what I want." And until you ask for it, it doesn't always know it. Your thoughts create form, but it is your emotional state that vibrates it into being. Your emotions are the engine for creation.

Q: So if someone wanted more money in their life, but they always felt anxiety about money, that fear would keep it away?

A: Yes, because the signal you're sending out on an emotional level is "I'm afraid of it." You may have that thought once or twice—that you feel like you want it while that underlying fear is constant. That's the signal that's being sent out. It all comes down to judgment, always. You're holding on to judgment of some sort. It may be what money represents. If it's "the wealthy are corrupt," then that's the thought form you've got there. You've got judgments about that. Or you could have a judgment that you don't really deserve it. There are lots of different reasons why, where the core issue could be, and when you're talking about money in particular, when we look at humanity there are usually multiple reasons. You have been

> *Your thoughts create form, but it is your emotional state that vibrates it into being.*

conditioned and you've got a lot to unplug from, from mass consciousness.

Q: When the judgments and core issues come up, how do you clear them?

A: One is just by not judging. It is seeing how these situations are of service. When you can see what you've learned or why a situation has been presented, then you can release your judgment about it. Let us give you an example. If you are afraid of power, you're going to put yourself in situations to test your power or for others to subjugate you so that you can learn that you have personal power. There are no victims here. There are only willing participants. So when you are the recipient of that domination, in other words when you are allowing others to subjugate you, the moment you stop you see that you have power.

So the whole thing is set up. This reality is showing you that you have power. Now, you've got to clear the issue that's at the heart of it, of why you were afraid to use your power. But the incident itself was just a catalyst, an opportunity for you to see that within yourself. And when you can recognize it as being such, then it loses its charge. If you can begin to understand that others are playing that role so that you can see that about yourself, they're reflecting it for you, they are in service to you, that changes the dynamic of the relationship. They are no longer someone who is dominating you. They are someone who has agreed, on a soul level, contracted to serve you. To be of service to you, to help reflect this back to you. And that creates a very different emotional response, and it neutralizes that charge. It alters the frequency.

Q: Would that scenario apply to someone like Hitler and the people he put in prison camps?

A: We're talking about a larger event, but yes. As a mass consciousness, to alter that perception of who they are and what they hold to be important. That being who was Hitler agreed to be of service to that collective, to that group, to that genetic line. And that's a hard one for humans to see. That's a very hard thing for them to begin to forgive. And then that goes back to the veil and why the veil was placed there, here, so that you don't remember everything. Because this has played itself out before in more dramatic ways that have created far more strife than what has happened on this planet, which is hard to imagine because you've had so much bloodshed, so much pain. Entire star systems have been destroyed.

All that is stored within you energetically, and it's also stored in that genetic line. It's part of what they wanted to heal. So they wanted to go through the experience again in order to bring it up, just as you're doing now on a personal level as you work through things in your life and then start to clear through past lives.

Q: It's all quite complex, but in a way it also feels simple.

A: Yes, it really is a lot easier than you imagine it to be. The universe is a rather simple place. But the mind, the intellect, makes it far more complex.

Q: To make our way in the universe, what are the basics a person should know?

A: One is that you have free will. Two, that there are only willing participants. There are no victims. So you can create your reality. You can unplug from mass consciousness and create a separate reality. And this is all an illusion; it is all an illusion. You are an immortal being who has chosen to project itself into this game. It's a bit like watching a film. It's an illusion. It's like watching a play at the theater, actors who have donned roles. In an improvisation, they have things they want to sketch out, and then they go for it. They start to move through this scenario. That's what you're doing down here.

Q: So if one wants to change his reality, what are the basics he needs to do?

A: Start working with your fears, facing your fears. You know when you've got a fear. Many of you are quite aware of it and decide, "you know, I really don't want to look at that." And so you don't. You know what we're talking about, there are times when you feel yourself tense up, and you're conscious of it. So it is a choice. Society will tell you that you have to do X, Y, and Z in order to achieve a particular result, and we'll tell you that's not true. What has to be is that your vibrational state has to be in alignment.

We always say it's a little bit like placing your order with the universe, if you will. You climb the stairs to the rooftop of the building and you throw your boomerang out to the universe. That's your order. You've taken yourself to a frequency level up here. So you place your order, then you begin to worry about it. "It hasn't come back yet, I must not deserve it, I'm not going to get it." So you drop yourself out, you go down a couple floors. Well, then the order comes back, and you're not standing on the roof anymore. You've dropped out of the frequency range that that exists in. So you've got to keep yourself at the rate at which you are placing your order. That's how that works.

Q: What do you do about those nagging doubts that come in after you place your order? Is that related to fear?

A: Yes. Usually it's trust in the universe. Trusting that you can have what you want. And where does that notion that you can't have what you want come from?

Q: Parents, teachers, religion.

A: Yes. Well, you know your parents set it all up for you. They set up all the hurdles, that's why you chose them. All of the conditioning. They help you to create all the obstacles that you then get to move through. That's part of the joy of parenting. And you do the same thing for your children.

Q: So we shouldn't have any resentment against our parents?

A: No, you knew full-well what you were walking into. You chose them. You knew all of their quirks, all of their belief systems that you were going to take on. Without exception. There's no point in blaming them. Again, no victims, only willing participants.

Q: There's a lot of talk these days about the Law of Attraction. What's your take on that?

A: We will tell you, thought creates form. But your emotional states vibrate it into being. Whatever you are putting out emotionally you're going to get back energetically. And because the physical reality is reflecting the emotional, if they're lower frequencies that you're putting out, then what you're getting back in the physical realm are the lower frequencies, the events that are in sync with that vibration. Again, it's all about energy, and you match that vibration, that vibratory rate. There are many beings out there talking

> *The most toxic thing you do to the planet is to generate your negative emotions.*

about the Law of Attraction, and we're very happy to see that it has reached mass consciousness.

The next law that you're going to start to comprehend is that you're holographic in nature. As above, so below. When you really understand that one, that's when you can make major changes in the planet. We will tell you global warming is not man-made, not at the level you are being told. It is part of a natural ascension process. Your sun is undergoing changes as well. Yet having said that, we feel it is important that you begin to work in harmony with the planet and other beings on it, the other species on the planet. The most toxic thing you do to the planet is to generate your negative emotions. If you look at the state of health of the individuals on this planet, it's not very high. And because you're holographic in nature, guess what, neither is the planet's. It's very toxic right now. Because beings are toxic, a lot of their thoughts are very toxic.

But you're changing. The planet tries to keep up, she tries to clear herself and create a balance, and sometimes that means dramatic events: maybe volcanic eruptions, maybe tidal waves, maybe earthquakes. All those things are ways for the planet to process the emotional energy that you're generating and to release it, to transmute it. Just as you may generate a cold in your body. The cold is just helping to process energy out of your body.

Q: I'm a little confused about something. You said the dark is as necessary as the light, yet the negative thoughts are causing the toxicity. So what is the role of negative thought?

A: It's for you to release. There is some judgment being held there that is creating the negative thought. Even in some of the "light" thoughts, there's judgment held there. But we're focused on the other end more often than not because of the frequency. And even if you're thinking "light" thoughts, it could be how you feel about others. You may be someone who is working to clear yourself and you are judging others who are not doing the same. That "My way is best. Look how good I am. Look how well I am doing with a particular way of eating." There's lots of judgment held on that, and it is not healthy. When we talk about the negative, about emotion, it's more of a lower frequency than a negative frequency. Perhaps we should rephrase that for you. It's the lower frequencies we're trying to alter.

Q: What is your definition of God?

A: Love. Source. But that word holds many connotations, and unfortunately many negative ones for this planet, because of how you've been conditioned with religion. You've been sold a lot of lies. But there's also a lot of truth in there. And you know if you want people to believe something that you're selling and it's not the truth, you're going to sprinkle it with the truth because if you told someone a bold-faced lie, guess what, they'd know you were lying. So there's a lot of conditioning you are dealing with. But a lot of things are being transmuted and altered at this time. You're finding out some things about some of your religious leaders, you're finding out some things about religion, that just don't hold true to you, aren't ringing true to you anymore. Because you're moving outside of that construct. You're moving toward a multidimensional state, you're remembering who and what you are and it doesn't need an intermediary.

Q: Since we are immortal beings, why are so many humans afraid of death?

A: That goes back to conditioning as well. It's just the way the game was set up. But there are more and more of you who are awakening and remembering that you are immortal beings. So that is changing.

Q: I wanted to know if you could give us some general information about what the human diet should consist of.

A: It's very simple, it all comes down to energy. There is no one right or wrong diet to follow. It depends on what your body needs at the time, because going through this process there are certain chemical needs. So eating an all-vegetarian or all-vegan diet is not always appropriate. If you're not ready to deal with an emotional issue, chances are your diet is not going to be very good. When you start to eat healthily, it starts to lighten your frequency. So you're not numb anymore, and emotional issues start coming to the surface. So if you don't want to deal with those issues, you're not going to eat healthy. If you feel that having something is unhealthy or it's going to create a negative response.

In other words, it's going to make you fat if you eat that cookie, and what you set up is a pattern of deprivation for yourself, and it depresses your system. The longer that goes on, the more damage it does energetically. If you actually had that cookie, it would take less energy to process it out of your body and for your body to recover energetically than it does for you to recover energetically from that emotional response. How you *feel* about what you're putting in is more important than *what* you're putting in. If you hold judgment on what you're eating, then it doesn't really matter what's going in. Because your body can process all of that.

It all goes back to the emotions. Because the emotional body creates the physical reality. So if you're talking about weight and health, how you are feeling about yourself is determining your physical body more so than what you're consuming and how you're exercising. Which is a very different way of thinking for many of you. Because you're conditioned to think that it's all physical. But it's not. It's all emotional. It all starts in the emotional body.

Q: It seems like people are trying to fill some kind of hole in themselves with drinking and drugs. What is that hole?

A: It's trying to connect with source energy. In order to connect they are picking up all this residual energy, all of this pain. Many of these beings are taking on energy from other people. They're taking on the ills of the world. It's stepping through it and seeing that that was the necessary experience of others, they're not moving through that stage. Do you understand? Does that make sense?

Q: Yes.

A: It's not that they're not capable of connecting, it's that they almost connect too much and are shutting down. Once you get on that cycle, it becomes more and more difficult to get out because there is also the chemical dependency to it all.

Q: What's the best way to heal an addiction?

A: Working on self-love and forgiveness. Because a lot of times there's also a judgment. A lot of times people don't want to feel because of a lot of judgment they've got about themselves. And it's interesting—it's much easier for you all to connect and to forgive others than it is to forgive yourselves, which sometimes is a hard concept to grasp. It may also be difficult to forgive someone else. They may have done something very dastardly. But it's even more challenging for many of you to forgive yourselves. You can forgive them, but you still can't forgive you.

Q: How do you get to that place where you can forgive yourself?

A: One step at a time. Changing those frequencies, changing those thought forms, looking at all those little incidents that built up to that. "So I've created this big event, why? So that I could see that I have power or so that I can see that

I am a sensitive being or whatever the issues are." If you're creating a big event, it's not the first time that this frequency has shown itself. It's shown itself repeatedly. Because that's also how it works, you are creating events, and you create them at low levels, and each time you suppress them, they get bigger and bigger and bigger. Events rarely come as one big event—usually there's a buildup. If you're getting a big event, usually it's a past life that is playing on it. If you've got a big event, like you've hit rock bottom, or you got a DUI, there's an underlying issue you're trying to get your attention to deal with.

Q: So it really doesn't serve us to suppress things?

A: Not at all. Face it and deal with it, and the sooner you deal with it, the easier it is. One, to deal with, because it's going to come back and get bigger. Just nip it in the bud, because if you think of all the wasted energy that goes into you worrying about something or something nagging at you telling you that you've got to do it—if you'd just done it in the first place it would be behind you.

Q: Wrapping up, is there anything you'd like to add?

A: Oh there's so much to cover, dear. Let us just say that you've got a lot of support energetically. You are going to find over the coming year or two that things begin to intensify. In your personal lives as well as in what's going on with the planet. And it's very important for you to see the planet as a healthy planet. Because when you continue to see her as damaged or you continue to see her as ill, that's what you create because it's what you're focused on. So it's vitally important that you begin to see yourselves as healthy and healing and see the planet the same. So when these events start to transpire, when you start seeing these challenges presented to you, these opportunities to clear, see them as opportunities to clear rather than "I'm doing something wrong, look what's come back." That's a very different perspective of reality, and they create two very different results. There are a lot of people out there talking about it right now. Out of those, take the bits and pieces that resonate with you, and you'll be fine. Trust your instincts.

Q: Could you be a little more detailed about the type of intensities we might face?

A: I don't want to go into too much detail because as we present information to you it alters your timeline. If we tell you something will happen, you will focus on it. And the moment we tell you, it alters the probability. It's different when you get information from a third-dimensional medium or a psychic who is incarnated into your system, because they are part of the game. We are not participating at the same level. So for us to give you that information affects you differently. We have a different perspective of the information as opposed to a psychic, who's picking up from within the game as part of the game.

> *It's vitally important that you begin to see yourselves as healthy and healing and see the planet the same.*

There may be some changes in governmental structures, but that really is as far as we want to go. And don't worry, it's just part of the cycle, and part of it is creating a different reality, it's allowing you to create a different reality. Structures sometimes have to fall apart so you can build a new foundation. Don't perceive things as falling apart, see them as building anew. Shift your perspective.

Q: What is your perspective on President Bush?

A: There are different perspectives, but let us say this . . . Many of you have a lot of animosity toward him and his actions, and we understand that. He is playing a role. If you are seeing this being and you're not happy with what he is doing, try to see the higher perspective. Imagine yourself as a being with millions of others sending hate and anger at you. Takes a very special being to be able to handle all of that. He is playing a necessary part for others. If you can see the role that he's playing, it is much easier to accept some of the things he is doing without hating him or being angered by him. And that relieves you of the burden of judgment. See the role that he's playing. There are a lot of beings out there doing things that are not of the highest frequency, and they play their part.

Q: Will our next president be more enlightened?

A: No. Because it's the same structure. It's the same governmental structure. It has the same ills. That's also being controlled and manipulated by the Annunaki. Those who are in power. It's part of the game. It's like putting a new tire on an old car—it really doesn't change the car, does it? Changing presidents is like changing a tire. It's still the same vehicle, and the vehicle is still driving on the same road.

Q: When do we get beyond that?

A: When you shift your own frequency. Because your governmental structures aren't going with you, you're creating a new version of how you want to govern. You're going to find the new way, and it's working internally. It's all working holographically.

Q: Who are the Illuminati?

A: Those who are aware of your history. Many of them are reincarnated dark priests of Atlantis. They are still playing that same game of power, understanding how things are connected and not utilizing that knowledge for the betterment of the globe or in a conscious way for the rest of humanity, the planet, or the other species on it.

Q: Can you give us any specific names of members of the Illuminati?

A: We could, but that wouldn't serve you. We would rather you focus on the fact that they're aware. But you know what? You are getting all the information as well. It doesn't really matter what the Illuminati are up to. They will keep playing their game even if you don't participate. The different versions of the planet will separate, and you'll be standing on this one, because you're vibrating up here. Their vibration is not changing, unfortunately. They are locked in that frequency. They're still working with that same mentality while they have the knowledge and the understanding of history and the understanding that you are part of a galactic community. They are still working for power; that spiritual growth has not come. And that's what's happening for you. You are now remembering who and what you are, you're also growing, and that's what's different.

Q: Do you have some uplifting final words for us?

A: You're always connected. You are all able to connect with your own guides; you are all able to be connected with source energy. And now that you have felt our frequency, you can connect with us. You don't need an intermediary, you don't need a channel—all you need to do is ask for assistance. You know, you all are beautiful beings of light. And we are very honored to have the opportunity to speak to you or to work with you. You really are very special and very rare. It took a lot of courage to come down to this system at this time. It's not an easy one to incarnate to, and many beings incarnate and walk right back out. They get here and say, "what was I thinking?" It is very dense down here.

This planet has some very beautiful things on it, and the range and expression of love is amazing and it is like no place else in the universe. You may say, "how is that possible, isn't love love?" There are lots of different shades and different kinds. The kind you have with a friend. The kind you have with a lover. The kind you have with a lifelong mate. With your brother, with your mother, with your father, they're varying shades, and that is what is so special about the love on this planet. It's not like that everywhere.

So enjoy that, enjoy the things that the planet has to offer, and relax. Have fun. Enjoy the ride. That's one thing we could leave you with—we recommend that what you do is that you enjoy life. Live it to the fullest. And know that we're always here. If you need us, you can call on us, and you don't need an intermediary. We will do our best to assist you and make sure you get the information that you are seeking. As long as you are asking, we will put it on your path, until you get it or no longer want it. So we'll be watching and waiting, dears, and sending many well-wishes.

Q: Thank you.

A: It has been our pleasure, dear.

≡

When Wendy came out of trance, she seemed slightly loopy, as if she'd taken an extra spoonful of cough medicine. She explained that it takes just a few minutes to get "regrounded," but that she always feels refreshed and like "melted love" after a session.

"I feel so blessed to be able to do this," she said. "It helps so many others and it's of great benefit to me as well."

Afterward, out on the street as we loaded equipment into Matt's car, he commented that I was one big smile.

"Yeah, I just love this!" I said. "It really lights me up from the inside out. I could have talked with them for hours more. It's just so great! Questions I've had my entire life are being answered in ways that actually make sense. What did you think?"

"Astonishing, that's about the only way I can describe it," he said. "All the answers were smooth and detailed, but the energy in the room was so much different compared to the first shoot. I guess these entities are beyond gender, or sort of a combination. But Bashar felt really masculine; the Pleiadians were gentler, more feminine.

> *The different versions of the planet will separate, and you'll be standing on this one, because you're vibrating up here.*

"Man, I'm really so happy I got involved with this project. So who's next?"

Three

Geoffrey Hoppe
Channeling Tobias

A week later, and just two weeks before Christmas, we took a flight from balmy, smog-shrouded Los Angeles to wintry Denver and its bleak, slate sky. Walking in the rental car lot, Matt and I were blasted by gusts of icy air. I said something along the lines of "this sucks." In fact, my exact quote, if memory serves, was "This sucks."

Canadian Matt just gave me a genuine smile and said, "That's so American of you. Always something to complain about, right?" He wasn't taking a real dig or being malevolent, and I smiled back because I realized he was right.

We headed up the mountain in our white Chevy Malibu (aren't rental cars *required* to be white?), discovered that we had a mutual love of Springsteen, and cranked the tunes.

An hour later, as a pink dusk segued to darkness, we arrived in the quaint mountain hamlet of Coal Creek Canyon—population 2,500—to meet with one Geoffrey Hoppe, the channeler we were to interview.

We checked into the only motel in town, the Eldora Lodge, all redwood and icicles. I noticed a hot tub outside on the huge deck and asked the owner if the water was heated now in the dead of winter. He said it was and we were free to use it anytime, day or night, which sounded like a plan for later, despite the temperature being 17 degrees.

When Geoff picked us up a few minutes later, I was struck by his gentle nature and youthful appearance. He was fifty-two, but easily could have been a decade younger. He packed us and our equipment into his SUV and drove us over snow-packed roads. We arrived a few miles later at the spacious home he shares with wife, Linda, his high school sweetheart.

After some small talk and a snack, we set up the filming equipment in the homey living room, fire crackling in the fireplace, snowflakes the size of quarters wafting outside. It could have been a Norman Rockwell painting . . . except for that fact that in a few minutes an "angelic being," as Hoppe likes to describe Tobias, would inhabit his body. But first we'd talk about how he got involved in channeling.

Geoff eased into a comfy chair and Linda sat nearby. I was slightly concerned that Geoff wanted her to be filmed alongside him, but he explained that her presence nearby and "her energy" are part of the channeling process for him. She's always with him now, but that wasn't always the case.

"For about a year I didn't even tell Linda that this voice had been talking to me in my head, a voice that was distinctly not my own," he said with a chuckle. "I didn't tell anyone, not even my own wife, because I thought people would think I was crazy."

A successful businessman at the time, Geoff said he was on an airplane during a work trip when "Tobias started talking to me, and hasn't stopped since." This was 1997, and two years later, after he'd had some practice and gotten used to the idea, he began to channel for small groups. "I started working with a psychologist who had some tough clients," said Hoppe. "You know, people with difficult issues. And it would be the psychologist, myself, and of course Tobias, and I really enjoyed that. It was dealing one on one in a very intense way. After word about that got out, then people wanted to do it in a group."

Linda interjected with a little smile, "You, the psychologist, Tobias, and a *client.*"

"And a client—right, right," he said. "And it's now grown into what it is."

Which is a global enterprise. Not only do the Hoppes put in more than a hundred thousand miles each year traveling the world for lectures and seminars, but also, they have now certified more than two hundred people to teach the "Crimson Circle" material.

"It has gone way beyond anything I'd ever envisioned, and it keeps growing," Geoff said. "So many folks out there are struggling with this shift, this ascension process, and often don't even know what's going on. So the channeling really helps bring them relief and answers."

After a short break, we all returned to our places in front of the camera. Geoff was ready to allow his non-physical friend Tobias to come through.

"Tobias is an angelic being who has lived many lifetimes on Earth," explained Geoff. "He is most noted for his lifetime as Tobit, one of the main characters in the book of Tobit from the Catholic Bible. His last lifetime on Earth ended in approximately 50 BC, and he comes back now through the angelic realms for what he calls the 'biggest evolution of consciousness humanity has ever experienced.'"

Quite a buildup, and I was now itching to speak with him. So Geoff closed his eyes and took several deep breaths as Linda softly encouraged him to relax and let his humanness fade out. The breathing continued for perhaps thirty seconds, punctuated by slight facial tics (but none as pronounced as Anka bringing forth Bashar).

Then Geoff's mouth opened and the words "And so it is" came out. The voice was essentially the same, perhaps an octave lower, but the energy in the room had shifted substantially.

During the first few minutes, I felt light-headed and like moths were fluttering in the pit of my stomach. And I felt excited, as if being reunited with a long-lost friend or perhaps an older brother who was sitting me down and trying to get across just what he'd learned so I wouldn't make the same mistakes. In any case, the conversation felt quite personal to me, more so than the first two interviews. Tobias was genial and accommodating, though at times did not mince words.

≣

Q: Hello Tobias, thank you for joining us.

A: Thank you. I'm going to take just a moment here as we bring all our energies in just to truly feel the surroundings here. We love it when the humans invite us in as you're doing now, particularly in such a warm and open space. It has been a while since I, Tobias, have been in the living room of Cauldre [that's the name that Tobias calls Hoppe] and Linda. I'm feeling the energy here. I'm looking at the painting of course of Cauldre and Linda and all of Shaumbra [the Crimson Circle followers] and wondering where my picture is that used to be hanging there. When the human allows us to come in this close, we have to do it by permission you see—they have to truly let us come in. Then we can feel through them, through each one of you sitting here, we can breathe in the energy in a way we can't do otherwise, so we're just cherishing this moment that we have with you. So let us begin with the discussion.

Q: Could you tell us about yourself, some biographical data and your history?

A: I have lived on Earth over one thousand lifetimes. I have lived back in the days of Lemuria; I have lived many, many lifetimes back in the time of Atlantis, perhaps some of my favorites; although I would have to say that your times now, your modern times, are much more dynamic, much more energized, than even in the times of Atlantis. I have lived in the more recent era, up to the times of Yeshua, the one you call Jesus. My last human lifetime was about fifty years before Yeshua walked on Earth. That is when I died in my last lifetime in the lands of Israel. And that is when I agreed not to come back for other lifetimes so that I could work with and assist humans, who I call Shaumbra, as they go through their own spiritual transformation process. I'm called Tobias because that is perhaps my most notorious and famous lifetime. It became one of the books of holy scripture, the book of Tobit. And that occurred about 600 years BC, when I was known as Tobit. I would encourage all of you to read the story; it's quite beautiful. It is hardly true, it was embellished through the years, but it makes a wonderful story.

I have had many, many lifetimes on Earth. I have deep love and compassion for humans because I remember what it was like to go through the things that humans are going through now. I remember one challenge in particular—the challenge of knowing at some deep level that you are a spiritual being. But when you come to Earth and you embody yourself in this thing called biology, your physical body, and you have then a brain—you see, angels don't have brains, thank God—but when you descend your energy into the physical, you tend to lose the remembrance of who you truly are. You forget that you are an angel. You forget that you are not limited.

You get very focused in your everyday, conventional life. I have great compassion for what humans go through every day. So many of you I know personally. We have shared lifetimes together. So many of you who call out and pray out, I come to your side along with other angels who are helping to work with you. I work with your spirit and your soul, as you as a human and an angel are going through your transformation process. So that is my brief story.

Like all of you, prior to coming to Earth I was an angel, a nonphysical being you might say. I had tremendous experiences in the other realms as well, but I would have to say there is nothing—even in the angelic realms—nothing like the human experience.

Q: Tobias, why do we choose to have this amnesia when we come to Earth, and why do we do it so many times, over and over?

A: The amnesia that you refer to, the forgetting that you are an angel and why you ever chose to come here in the first place, it is a result of being here on Earth. There is this intense density in matter here that creates this. In the other realms we don't have trees that you can smash your cars into, and we don't have buildings that you have to live in. Everything is so focused energetically here. There is a gravity—not the typical Earth gravity that you know, it is more of an energetic gravity—that concentrates and compacts the energy so tightly that when your spiritual energy descends into this realm it causes a type of forgetfulness. It is not necessarily by choice, it is a matter of spiritual physics that it happens. Part of it, I guess you could say, is a good thing because it allows each of you to truly experience what it is like to live in an illusion. An illusion that you're all creating together through mass consciousness and through your belief systems. It allows you to be so immersed in this illusion that it is more real than real itself. It has more truth in it than truth in the angelic realms. It is so "here" and so "now" that it gives you the absolute fullest experience.

The downside is that you get lost in it and you get trapped in it. You feel there is absolutely no way out. You become so frustrated and angry that you actually dig yourself deeper into this 3D reality. Because you then get into your mind. The mind is such an important component of living on Earth, but it is vastly overrated. The mind does wonderful things, but for so many people it keeps you from using your higher consciousness, your divine intelligence, as we call it. So you get stuck here, you get lost like a child in the woods, thinking that nobody knows where you are or cares that you're there. Thinking that you are off in this dark, potentially dangerous space, and can never get out. That is probably one of the greatest fears that people have, that there is no way out of this. Whether you believe in one lifetime or you believe in reincarnation, there's a deep-seated fear within humans that they're not going to get out. That causes things like anxiety and depression, schizophrenia, and all these other mental diseases that you see in your societies right now.

Humans get very lost—they don't know the way out and they get even more trapped. They get into this belief system that there is no way out, and that belief system literally keeps pulling them back to Earth for another cycle of reincarnation after reincarnation after reincarnation. Even when there is no need for karma, there is no need to come back here to Earth anymore, they keep coming back. They're into such a rut or routine or habit, and you combine that with the emotional connections they have with other humans, wanting to come back to be with them in another lifetime or feeling that they have to. And now indeed you have a situation where they are desperate. They are hurting, in pain, but they don't know how to get out. There are many levels of angelic beings working with humans right now, but it is difficult because even if we have been at your side in the past, there are times when you're not listening. We're communicating that you are indeed God also, you're living in a type of illusion, an illusion that presents itself like a matrix of human consciousness that keeps you trapped in it.

How do you get out? You get out by getting so into it, you see. By loving life, by loving yourself, by accepting all things as they are. By accepting everything about yourself, not just a few things but everything. As you learn to have that deep compassion for yourself and deep compassion for other humans, as you learn to truly embody in life and find joy in everything—even what you would call the dark parts of life, they're not dark, they're just different—as you come to understand the total joy of life, that is how you get out. You don't get out by praying your way out, you definitely don't get out by just doing good deeds for others, because then you're not really doing it for yourself, you don't get any kind of brownie points on the other side. There are no tricks to it; you don't have to be a Houdini to get out.

You just realize that life is a precious gift. And life continues after you leave this planet, after you leave the physical body. But now because you've learned to appreciate, enjoy, and love yourself and life, you take a different perspective with you when you depart this Earth and go on to the other realms.

Q: What about people who have difficulty loving themselves and getting joy out of life, are there certain steps they can take?

A: I'm going to simplify this for you. And perhaps some may think the answer is a bit terse, but: Just get over it. You're wallowing in your own self-pity, you've set up an energy of being a victim. A victim of life, a victim of other people. You're allowing them to steal your energy and to steal your heart and your consciousness. You're in a type of trap, and you're letting it happen. You decide one day when you're getting out of bed or one night when you're taking a walk that you're just going to get over it. You're going to stop letting others take from you, and you're going to stop taking from other people as well. You're going to be whole and sovereign. It is truly that simple.

What makes it complex and makes it difficult for humans is they develop all these multistep programs, and they write books, and they have seminars and classes and they get more and more and more into the mind and away from the true matter at hand. You are an angelic being. You are God also. Get over all the rest of it. It sounds a bit terse, but it is perhaps the most effective thing we've found. You are the Creator. You've created things you like and don't like in your life, and if you created them, you can also un-create them.

The important thing here is to make a choice. Oh, you say

that you have made choices. I'm going to contest that. I'm going to say that you have wants and desires, that you wish things would be a certain way, but you haven't proclaimed to yourself, to your soul and to your body and to your mind, that you are going to take the path of higher consciousness. Why? Because you're afraid. You know that you can get by. And that is one of my problems with humans on Earth right now. I call it "just enough"—just getting by, enough money to just live, enough health to just get by, just enough. When you proclaim to yourself that you are God also and you feel it deep within you, not just from your head, but you proclaim it to yourself that you are God, you are your own creator and you don't need to take energy from anywhere else, from anyone else, your life will change. It will change.

When your life changes like that, don't be surprised at the changes. That's one thing that always amazes the angelic beings that I work with. A human asks for change and then their life starts changing and then they—what do you call it?—freak out. Because they lose their job or they lose their family or they lose all that old baggage they've been carrying around. They go into fear. But understand that as these changes begin there's an evolution of energy. It is a cleaning house, getting rid of the old to make way for the new you.

Q: It seems like you're saying it's a choice of defining who you are rather than setting goals.

A: No goals. That is so mental, that is so yesterday—so '80s, Cauldre is telling us. Forget the goals. It is an exercise in frustration and futility. You, a sovereign being, don't need goals. Do you know why? I'll tell you why. Because you attract everything to you. When you make choices, you literally re-energize yourself. Think of yourself as a type of magnet or an attracting kind of energy. When you make choices in your life, you attract all the energies to you. We say to humans that all energy is there to serve you, it seeks to serve you, and the master allows energy to serve them. They understand it's there to serve them.

So throw out all the goals, throw out all the visualizations, throw out all the affirmations, because they don't work in the end. Oh, short-term results? Possibly. Long term they don't work. You're going to get stuck, and then you're going to go on medication. And that is where it is very difficult to talk to any of you once you are on those psychotropic drugs. Very difficult, because now you're a zombie. Your spirit exists somewhere else, it's not present here. Those drugs knock your spirit out of this reality.

> *You are an angelic being. You are God also. Get over all the rest of it.*

Q: That's a blanket statement in all cases?

A: All cases.

Q: There's been a lot of talk about the Law of Attraction. What is your take on that?

A: The Law of Attraction works. Where it is becoming distorted right now is that it's turning into a mental exercise. Somebody out there wants to write a book, hundreds of pages outlining it. And then the moment the human starts to read that book they go mental and then it shuts down, you see. The mind can only go so far. The Law of Attraction is your spirit, your soul. It is the deepest parts of you; it's not what the brain can conjure up. It is the deepest parts of you.

There is a misunderstanding also about the Law of Attraction. The human, the limited human, uses it like this . . . "I want a new car." And they expect it to come to them. Well, it will . . . but it will probably hit them and send them flying.

The limited human says "I need one thousand dollars. I have to be able to pay my rent." You have a conflict going on now between the limited human and the souled being. The Law of Attraction works on, let us say, a soul level or a spirit level. I'm going to make another brash statement here. Your soul doesn't really necessarily care about all of the human whinings. The human gets so caught in the things it thinks it needs and thinks it has to have, but at the end of the day none of it matters.

It doesn't matter if you didn't pay your rent, it doesn't matter if you were a multimillionaire. None of it matters. Those are things of concern to the human aspect only. What the soul cares about, what your spirit cares about, is consciousness—which means awareness. Your soul and your spirit care about the joy of being. The joy of being. In other words, experiencing what is in front of you to experience. The soul would rather have a bad experience for you than no experience at all, you see. Those humans who try to run from experiencing things and doing things and creating things are really frustrating their own soul.

The soul comes back and throws a few what you would call "interesting events" into their life to get them awakened, and then the human complains and becomes even more of a victim. The Law of Attraction works when you are in your own safe sacred space, when you understand that all your supposed needs and desires as a human—in other words, basically to have something to eat, to stay relatively warm, and to have some kind of shelter and clothing—these are taken care of so easily and naturally. Ask any of what you call the human masters. Ask those who understand what it's like to be in their consciousness. You don't have to worry about the small stuff.

But the vast, vast majority, unfortunately majority, of

humans spend their valuable and precious creative energies chasing after the little things. That is why so often the difficult things happen in their lives. The spirit, the soul part of them, is trying to get their attention, saying you don't have to waste your energy on that, it will come to you naturally. The Law of Attraction works when you apply it to the higher consciousness aspects. The spirit aspects of your life. Aspects such as the growth and evolution of the soul. Learning about things like loving yourself, compassion for yourself. That is infinitely more important than a paycheck or a car.

You see, there's this conflict, a battle going on, in a way, between the human aspect and the soul self of you. The soul self is trying to say those things don't matter, these shall be taken care of by the spirit, by the I Am. If you ever stop running through that maze of human limitations, if you stop for a moment, your soul is saying to you, "listen, and be with me and allow me to come into your life and participate rather than pretending that I exist somewhere else. Or that I am some perfect kind of being sitting on a golden chair in some far-off reality." The soul is saying, "when you open your life to me, we will meld together once again. We will together know the joy of new consciousness, the joy of loving self, the joy of life. And then you won't have to sweat the small stuff."

Q: Is that what this period on Earth is about? What people call "the Great Shift," is it about the melding of spirit and human flesh in a sense?

A: It is indeed, and I'll expand on that even further. In the Lemurian age, which was the first age of humanity on Earth, it was about learning to bring your spirit energy into this realm on the Earth and embody it into physicality. Embody it into rocks and trees, but eventually evolving and learning how to put your energy into animals and living beings. So that first era in Lemuria was really about adapting to the 3D reality. In the Atlantean era it was truly about communal living. There was no consciousness of God, the term "God" was not even understood. It couldn't be discussed because it wasn't even a concept. Everything in Atlantis was about the good of the whole. There was no individuality. It was about working together as groups. You ate together, you slept together, you worked together; it was all done communally.

In the early period of Atlantis there wasn't anything that you would now call a name for "yourself," that came in the later days. In this more current era of humanity, starting perhaps approximately ten thousand years ago, as the human species began becoming more than these nomadic tribes that were wandering and began to settle, this is when the modern concept of God came to be. And so for the past ten thousand years or so it's been about a new understanding. Understanding that there is a type of God, a type of higher being. There was a responsibility to something else, that was the important thing. That has been the consciousness up until very, very recently.

The new consciousness right now is about the "I Am." And while to some it might sound very selfish, it is actually about discovering yourself. It is about putting yourself first, loving yourself first, taking care of yourself first, having compassion for yourself first, and knowing yourself first. Because as you do this, then and truly then you are able to help humans but, you understand, only humans who are choosing help. As you come into this era of I Am, it is also discovering that this God that humans have been seeking for the past ten thousand years doesn't exist up in heaven somewhere, isn't hidden somewhere, it is right here. It has always been there. That is what this new consciousness is all about.

Q: Considering that, how will it manifest? What will our world be like in the next few years?

A: Oh my God, if I knew that I would be a prophet. I have to say that this changeover from the old religious system that so many of you are familiar with is difficult, very difficult, because it holds on tightly. Those who have such a strong concept of God as some higher authority and the only creator, they want to hang on to that dearly. They will feel very uncomfortable letting that go for a variety of reasons. They fear letting God go—their old God you see. Because they are so out of touch with themselves that they can't possibly even contemplate what it's like to have to go inside. They're so used to going out there, within this belief they have that some God is controlling things. And if they appease God, they're going to have just enough in their life. So it is a substantial, major change in consciousness coming over Earth right now.

You have a large percent of the population that is deeply hypnotized into their old religious beliefs. You have another portion of the population that found no satisfaction, they didn't find answers or any sense of peace, from this concept that religions tout—so they've gone into their own type of nothingness. They don't believe in God, but they don't believe in themselves. These are the ones you might call the atheists. They are in a neutral space and perhaps they are content with their life, but their consciousness is suffocated right now.

There is a very, very small group of people on Earth right now who are doing some phenomenal internal work. It is very difficult work. It is the work of the transformation of their own consciousness. Opening up, understanding that God isn't out there, the soul isn't out there, it's all right here. This work that's being done by a small group on Earth right now is going to set up the potentials, and I underline "potentials" because they're not forcing or inflicting it on anyone; they're setting up the potentials for other humans who are ready to take that major leap. Crossing over the chasm to the discovery of the I Am. The difficult part is it requires letting go of the old God, of the old sense of limitation. That, I would say, is the most difficult challenge a human will ever go through.

Q: But don't humans want to be unlimited and powerful?

A: Oh, they want to be rich, they want to be good-looking, they don't want to have problems, but that in itself is a limitation. They don't know how to think beyond these very rudimentary concepts. They want to win the lottery. They want to not have to worry about paying their bills, and that is where human consciousness is right now.

Q: So what's some basic advice about how a human can take that leap?

> The discovery of the I Am . . . requires letting go of the old God, of the old sense of limitation.

A: Generally speaking, and perhaps sadly speaking, the human has to get to such a place of suffering or pain—they have to get to perhaps a near-death type of incident. They have to go through something traumatic like the death of a loved one or perhaps a divorce. They have to go through the loss of things in their life to shake 'em up and wake 'em up. They have to get to a place where they only have themselves. They've tried calling out, they've tried getting help from outside, whether it is an outside God or a group of humans, and it hasn't worked.

And then they have to go inside to see what they're made of. That is the dark night of the soul. That is the chasm that they cross. That is the point also, oddly enough, that what you would call the spirit guides, the angelic beings, they have to back away at that time. They have to let the human go through their experience on their own, because otherwise they wouldn't discover who they truly are. Very few humans are willing to do that. They're satisfied with just enough. They're satisfied with just getting by. And they have hopes of perhaps a brighter day, a wealthier day or a healthier day, but those hopes day after day after day seem to get crushed. They come to a point in their life where something happens traumatically. They say, "I'm going to look at it differently." Now mind you, it doesn't *have* to be this way, but that is the pattern that we see with humans. What we would say is love yourself. Take care of yourself. Learn to be with yourself. Go off and take a month, forty days perhaps as Yeshua did, go off by yourself and learn to be with *you*. Learn that you don't need to steal energy from anyone else, and don't let them do it to you. You're a sovereign, self-sustaining being.

> *Love yourself. Take care of yourself. Learn to be with yourself . . . You're a sovereign self-sustaining being.*

Q: So let's say someone appears to have a good life, lots of money, a good family—you're saying in some cases they might not have made this leap?

A: There is no direct parallel between having money and having this higher consciousness. Some people are very astute at making money. Some people are very good at taking money and energy from other people. Some humans are good at creating new things that other humans would be attracted to and pay for. But that doesn't necessarily equate to consciousness.

It is a funny thing when you come to the I Am consciousness within yourself and you realize that all things will be there for you. You don't need to be fabulously wealthy because you understand that, and this is a little difficult, you already are wealthy. You don't need to attain it or aspire to it. You don't need to set it as a goal, because it is already there. But a funny thing happens: It matters very little. That doesn't mean you have to walk around like a beggar, because why suffer on Earth if you're here? But it means it just doesn't matter. Those who understand this principle, what they find is it's just there. They don't have to track it or work it or force it—it just appears. They don't have to lie awake at night worrying about it. It is just there, in the moment that they need it. Everything is there as they need it.

Q: You mentioned Yeshua. Why do so many humans look at him as a savior of some sort?

A: It makes a good story. Humans need a hero. They need sports heroes, they need political heroes although there aren't many, they need technology and science heroes, but they also need an icon that they can look up to and worship because they don't go within. In the early days of the Catholic Church there was a basic understanding that Jesus would appeal to the masses because he was a human. And that he would be such a fine example. It took them well over five hundred years to decide amongst themselves how he would be presented to the public. In your modern terms it would be how his PR campaign would be handled. How they would tell the story. They watched and observed what the humans were drawn to and what they didn't like.

So they developed this very interesting but not necessarily accurate story of Jesus, which wasn't even his real name to begin with when he walked on Earth. It was Yeshua, Yeshua ben Joseph. So they need something outer, and they pray to Jesus. I have to say here, perhaps as a shock to some of you: Jesus is not a souled being. You will not find him in the other realms. Jesus is a manifestation of a group conscious- ness. So they need someone to look to and to worship, and their leaders even, religious leaders who have no idea what the I Am principle is about, who have no idea that God is already within, they encourage their groups to worship some far-off Jesus. Because it is a wonderful way of perhaps what you would call anesthetizing them a bit, taking their mind off their daily pain. But it is also a wonderful way of controlling. So whether it is the Christian Church or whether it is so many of the other religions, they create these icons. But the icons are out there somewhere, and they're generally hardly based in reality.

Q: Is the Christ consciousness present in every human?

A: The Christ consciousness is the sovereign being. It is a type of crystalline energy—but please understand that we're not just talking about your crystals that you have sitting on your dresser or your nightstand. We're talking about crystal being the clearest form of energy. An unbiased, untainted type of energy. It is the I Am principle, and it has become known as Christ consciousness. The crystal consciousness of yourself, indeed.

Q: There's been a lot of talk about 2012; is there any signifi- cance to that year?

A: As I see it, there will be some wonderful yields in the vineyards in that year around the country, making for some fine vintages. There will be a lot of headlines in the newspa- pers because it's drama. Humans feed on drama. If I could bottle drama and sell it I would be a millionaire—although I would have no use for the money.

Humans are going to focus on this event in 2012 and it's

going to create a certain drama and paranoia and there are going to be books coming out about it, and there are going to be workshops and schools and 2012 helmets that you can put on your head and all of these other things. And then it will come and go, and 2013 will be here. And then there's going to be a lot of sad and depressed humans. But oddly enough, these sad and depressed humans who have just been uninspired by 2012 and unchanged by it, they're going to go find another 2012, another guru, another date, another color, another *something* that they can look to outside of themselves. But one of these days—one of these days, maybe just enough humans will start remembering, letting themselves remember who they are, and that will inspire new consciousness on Earth.

Q: But aren't more and more people remembering who they are?

A: Not really. Actually this mass consciousness, what we call the hypnosis or the matrix, is getting heavier and heavier. And more and more humans are falling into the "just enough" syndrome. They're falling into this whole true lack of joy of life. It is not at all what we expected or would choose if we were them; however, the good news is that there are mavericks out there. There are those who are going outside of the grid. There are those who are taking huge leaps of consciousness within themselves, they are looking inside for the answers rather than letting somebody outside do it for them. They are going deep, deep within themselves to the point where it hurts on every level. To the point where they are breaking this pull, this type of magnetism from mass consciousness, and going off on their own.

As you can imagine this is a lonely journey, and because of the training of figuring everything out in the mind and analyzing only in the mind, they often get stuck in the mind. They get trapped there, bogged down there. They doubt themselves. They doubt all of the things that they truly feel about life and about themselves and about others. They doubt the inspiration that they get. Then they tend to get sucked back into the matrix. However there are enough humans right now on Earth who are breaking out. Who are looking within and understanding that they are sovereign. These standards of new consciousness and of the Christ consciousness energy you referred to, they are going to be the examples. They are going to be the examples to other humans that you can cross the chasm of old consciousness to new. That you can integrate the human and the divine right here, right now. You don't have to wait till you die to do it; you don't have to wait till your next incarnation. You can do it right here.

This small group of mavericks is going to show the way. You're not going to see that old type of guru dynamic you've seen in the past; they're going to remain very balanced and steady as standards or examples of new consciousness.

Q: I feel like I'm one of those.

A: And so therefore you are. You indeed know what it's like to be a maverick. You and I have had many, many talks. Long talks at night. I'm always amazed at how late you can stay up. But you also have that tendency then to doubt yourself.

Q: How can one deal with doubt and dismiss doubt once and for all?

A: It is as simple as going outside of the mind. Doubt works in the mind, it is a sister of the ancient "sexual energy virus." It gets you trapped in your mind. Imagine now you get into that place of doubting yourself, which is, granted, easy to do. But instead of noodling in your mind, instead of analyzing yourself, which is basically just judging yourself, instead of doing any of that, you go out of your mind. You go to your own expanded consciousness, you open up. And you say "mind, stop for a moment, take a vacation. I'm going to go to my higher level of consciousness." You do a bit of breathing, you stop the mind's chattering and churning. You open up and you remember, then it comes to you. You remember those inspired moments that you have. You remember why you came back here to Earth, you remember the talks that we've had even in your sleep state that you tend to forget when you wake up in the morning. As you open up to this new consciousness, you go beyond the mind and go beyond the doubt.

Q: You mentioned a sexual virus. Could you talk about that?

A: It is basically an old wound. It is an old energy imbalance. Anytime energy or consciousness is imbalanced, it will do anything to find its way back to balance—including things that may seem destructive and things that seem counterproductive. But if you stand back and look at it, the energies are just trying to rebalance. Going way back, long before Earth ever existed, there was a wound or a split in the masculine-feminine energy. I'm not talking about men and women; I'm talking aspects of yourself. With that energy split there was a wound, a sadness that has existed up until now. The way to bring that back together eventually was what we call the sexual energy virus. It is not about dealing with sex as you know it, the type of having sex with another for pleasure; it is talking about the nature of the masculine and feminine. The rift created a consciousness virus that is rampant on Earth right now. Sexual energy virus steals joy out of a person's life. Steals happiness.

It isn't owned by anybody, it's not part of a secret government, it's not controlled by dark forces in the angelic realms or any of that. It just is. The sexual energy virus gets into your life and affects it in a variety of ways, but the biggest factor is that it needs energy. It's going to steal it, and when it has taken enough energy from you, it's going to get you to then go out and rob it from other people to satisfy it, you see. So you're going to now go do things, perhaps play the role of a victim—the victim is one of the greatest robbers of energy there is. It's the "poor me" syndrome. All they're doing is stealing energy and consciousness from others. Then you find you are depleted so now you need to steal it from somebody else, they steal it from you, now you have this whole chain of events going on, unbeknownst to you consciously. It's just happening. It is very prevalent in society right now. It is perhaps one of the biggest issues. Ultimately it is about bringing back the masculine and feminine within you.

You see, you're not meant to be a split entity. You are not meant to have fragments of yourself unbeknownst to you all over the place. Indeed you can create aspects creatively, but you are conscious of them and you're aware of why they're there and know how to reintegrate them at any time. What we have right now is a situation where we have this split of the basic soul self. These two aspects, the masculine and feminine, are looking to come back together and through the work that many of you, and many of us in our realm, are doing, it is starting to happen. They are starting to reunite.

Q: What will help facilitate this reunification?

A: It boils down to self-love. Loving yourself. In the sexual energy school that we conduct, we go through a very intensive and transformational period. I do not want to give away the end of the story because it is important for humans, at least for right now, to go through this whole process. I can say it involves loving yourself, coming back to the point of absolutely loving who you are. Nothing else matters.

Q: Does loving yourself have to do with overcoming what parents have taught you that has become ingrained?

A: If you get into the type of analysis, if you start going into all the things that you learned and the hypnosis and the over-lays that have been placed on you or you've accepted into your own life, you're going to go mad. As many of the great masters have done, so there's potentially a value in going mad—but you don't have to do that. You don't have to go back and psychoanalyze yourself, which is a mental activity, or have a psychologist or psychiatrist do it for you. It is about making a choice. Waking up in the morning, taking a deep breath, making a conscious choice about loving yourself.

Try it tomorrow morning. Wake up, take a deep breath, say "today I'm going to love myself unconditionally and with grand compassion." You've just now changed your energy and your consciousness—your dynamic. Now immediately what's going to happen is there's going to be part of you that rejects this, that says you're playing a little game with yourself. "Who are you? Weren't you taught that it is wrong to love yourself? Isn't it narcissistic? Isn't it perhaps even evil? Wasn't that a stupid concept to love yourself?" And you're going to start this whole doubt process. So energies are going to come in to see how serious you are about loving yourself. They're going to challenge you, things inside of you and outside of you. The energy wants to know: Are you real or is this another game you're playing? Is this another class you've taken? Is this the affirmation of the month, or are you real? You're going to see energy start to change and shift immediately when you make this choice in yourself. Understand that part of it is just you testing you. Are you real?

On the other hand, it's also going to start immediately clearing away old energies. Old energies that represented a lack of love of yourself. You're going to go through a period of release. Release sometimes means you can lose things. If you have a lack-of-self-love job, you're going to lose that job. If you've taken a position only to make money, thinking that is what you have

> It boils down to . . . coming back to the point of absolutely loving who you are. Nothing else matters.

to do to get by, you're going to lose that job. Because it is not a self-love job. You're going to lose family members and friends because all of that old baggage, the energy that isn't compatible with yours, will fall away.

Q: If Earth life can be so painful and difficult—you say we get sucked back into it—but it's still our choice to come back, why do we keep doing it?

A: There's a variety of reasons. Some humans get sucked back into it because of trauma, and some get sucked in by karma. Let us take for example someone who is killed in battle in World War II. They left their body of course, went to the other realms. But there was so much what you call emotional or traumatic attraction that they feel like they left themselves back on Earth with many things unfinished, and oftentimes they are very angry. So they are literally sucked back into it. It's not like when they got to the other side they had all this grand consciousness and awareness. They still had very much the human consciousness. That human consciousness will get sucked right back in. There's an incredibly strong draw that Earth has. It didn't used to be that way.

But with so many humans having so many experiences and so much energy on Earth, it is like an incredibly strong magnet that pulls them back up until the point that the human self on Earth—not the soul being but the human self on Earth—finally says, "I've had enough, I want a different way," which sends out a type of clarion call to their spirit that says it's time for that soul to come in now. It's time for all the aspects of themselves to reunite. The clarion call goes out, and that starts this incredible transformation process.

The process doesn't necessarily occur in a year or two. Or a lifetime or two. For many humans it could take five, ten lifetimes to occur. It is a process. We're delighted that there are so many humans that we are working with right now, this group called Shaumbra, that are actually doing it—many of them—in a single lifetime.

Q: Isn't it true that in the new energy the process can be accelerated?

A: Absolutely. New energy provides more potentials than ever before and a different type of physics or a different dynamic than what has been available before. It is a deeper pool of your own consciousness that comes in, and the thing that makes it difficult is that it does not act like the old energy. Many humans are looking for new and improved old energy. A little bit easier, a little bit faster. What they haven't figured out yet is that it is totally new. It looks different, it smells different, it acts different. More than anything, new energy doesn't put itself into the dynamic of repeating itself—an aspect of old energy. New energy will be different each time you use it, even if you're using it for the exact same event or reason. It will be different each time. Humans get into patterns, and they expect things to respond or act the same generally each time they do it. New energy is totally different.

tuning in

Q: A term I've been hearing a lot recently is "lightworker." Can you comment on that and about what it is?

A: It is half. You have to be a lightworker and a dark worker. Lightworkers—those who are biased to the light only—are basically imbalanced. And sooner or later, then, they're going to have to experience their dark part, of which they're deathly afraid. They're afraid of that dark part within. Why do they label it dark? Why do they think it's evil? It's just another aspect of them.

We've said it before in some of our transmissions, that the darkness is actually your divinity. It is the part of you that loves you so much that it takes all your judgments and it takes all your doubts and all your shortcomings and everything you don't like about yourself and holds it for you. And then you play a game. You call yourself a lightworker like you're not going to even acknowledge that the dark exists—that *your* dark exists. But sooner or later you'll have to come to terms with it. It is an interesting dynamic, because some people who call themselves lightworkers run from the dark—they fear it. They think it has more power than they do. They also think they're going to earn their way into some strange heaven somewhere by going out and sprinkling fairy dust on all the humans around them. They're trying to save the world, but they've forgotten to save themselves. So we don't like to use that term "lightworker," even though we know the intention is generally good.

Q: You have also talked about ascension. What does that mean?

A: Ascension is when you finally accept the fact that you are God also. That you are that you are. That you're not trapped or limited in your human nature—when you understand that you're completely sovereign. That is ascension. When you understand that there is no God out there. When you don't need to appease some outside god or spirit or angels. Ascension is when you understand that you are your own One. There's this other concept that to me is getting quite long in the tooth, quite old. It is that we are all one. That was an old Atlantean concept. We're not all one. You are your own One. When you understand that and feel it—not just think it from the head, but when you truly understand that you are your own One—that is when you finally have grand compassion for everything else. You understand everyone else's journey. You understand that we all came from the same source but we are not some grand singular pool of oneness consciousness.

When you get to the point of ascension, you understand that you are God also. And then you see everybody else and everything else in a whole different way. You understand that they are still in the old concept of oneness and heaven-ness and God. And that is fine for them, but you've discovered that you are your own One. Now it sounds perhaps cold and impersonal, but I can tell you it actually is the grandest of all. That is the point when you truly understand how everything works.

> *Ascension is when you finally accept the fact that you are God also . . . That you are your own One . . . We're not all one. You are your own One.*

Q: Seems to me that people who get caught up in addictions and materialism are trying to fill some kind of hole in themselves. What is that hole and how best to fill it?

A: It's a couple things—part of it is just denial instead of again looking within for your own answers and your own fulfillment. People who have these addictions find short and temporary pleasure where they get to avoid really looking within. So it's an avoidance mechanism. But there's another aspect to it. This goes back to the Atlantean days when we were looking to conform and standardize the human body. We were looking to standardize the brain as well. So we weren't all different sizes and shapes; we were very, very communal. There was a time in Atlantis when some of the energies were becoming very imbalanced, and there were those in a position of leadership or control who literally embedded a type of pleasure center, an artificial pleasure center, into the human biology and into the mind as well. And it was a very effective tool back then because you could get someone to work very long and very hard—and really basically steal their energy—and give them just a little bit of pleasure. Back then it was pleasure that was derived from plants—similar to what you have today—and also the sexual pleasure.

So you could basically have a slave society and keep them as slaves without having to have iron around their wrists or their ankles because you're controlling them through this little pleasure center. That energy is carried forward even into the modern consciousness, so that accounts for the addictions. You're trying to continually trigger that pleasure center to give yourself just enough to get by.

Q: If life is a game, Tobias, why aren't people having more fun?

A: I wouldn't want to say that life is a game. Life is an illusion more than a game. Life is an experience, but not necessarily just something that's frivolous. Life can be enjoyed as a game—in other words you don't get so serious about things—but yet at the same time there is tremendous expansion of consciousness at every different level of you by living here on Earth.

Humans have gotten very mental. Humans have gotten to the point where they are continually looking outside, and this is a very potent recipe when you do this. Pretty soon what you have is people running around in circles. Even the leaders are running in that circle now. And what you have is a group of humans—a large group—who don't even know why they're running in the circle, who don't even understand why they've been doing it. They've been programmed to do it, and so they do it. At some point something triggers within that human—a tap on the spiritual shoulder, so to say—where they remember that there's more. They remember that there's got to be something else, and they desire more. And that's when the spiritual awakening begins. That's when they go from just being a human running in that circle now to a human running in the circle but also looking for the way out. That is what "the awakening" is about, and so many humans are starting to go through that right now.

Go beyond. Go crazy. Open up . . . your consciousness . . . Imagine yourself soaring in the angelic realms . . . and don't be afraid of what you're going to lose, because you didn't need it anyway.

But they have nowhere to look for the examples, nowhere to look for those to help them help themselves, you see. But there is a small group we keep referring to here—a small group of humans—who are doing this, who are going beyond.

Q: And these are "Shaumbra"? What does that word mean?

A: It is a word that means "group of us who are friends." We've been together before. We have such a deep love and desire for humanity that we'll use ourselves as processors of consciousness to try and create new potentials. To try to create more sovereign consciousness on Earth right now. We are all old friends who have been together before.

Q: In wrapping up, Tobias, are there any parting words you'd like to leave us with?

A: As we conclude this I'm going to say "go beyond." Go beyond. Go crazy. Open up your thoughts, open up your consciousness. It is taking place within you, but it is now about opening those doors of yourself. Allowing yourself to imagine again. How long has it been since you actually imagined? I'm not talking about a mental focus. I'm talking about imagination. Imagine yourself soaring in the angelic realms and—guess what—you have done that. Imagine yourself singing new songs, creating music, writing books, painting pictures. Imagine yourself waking up in the morning and looking forward to the day—not thinking about how you're going to get through the day. Open yourself up now, go beyond, and don't be afraid of what you're going to lose, because you didn't need it anyway. And so it is.

≡

Geoff came out of trance, rubbed his eyes, and gave us a little smile as he took his wife's hand. I glanced at Matt and saw a placid, warm look on his face. I felt an odd combination of relaxation and eagerness; I think the latter stemmed from the fact that I just wanted to go on chatting with Tobias. My old friend, it turns out.

By the time we returned to the charming Eldora, it was a bit past 10 PM. Matt and I cracked a couple beers and chewed over the evening's events. "There is so much information given in every one of these interviews," he said.

"It's sort of just rolling over me like a wave and I feel like I'm soaking it up, but that all of it will really only kick in later. I mean, I'm still sort of processing all that 'Hitler did a service' stuff from the first two interviews, and now Tobias says, 'You are God also.' Something special is going on here. And I'm really awed by how easily all this is coming together. I recently directed a feature in Canada, and it was one problem after another. But this has been all but effortless."

I concurred with Matt on all points. But neither of us seemed quite ready to truly get into processing proper that very moment. We weren't rabbinical students holed up in a stone-cold yeshiva. (Okay, the room *was* a bit chilly. But also slightly claustrophobic.) After all that consciousness-expanding with the Hoppes and Tobias, we needed to get out.

I took the wheel of the Malibu, and we headed toward the nearest watering hole, a country bar some twenty miles away. The road there featured the very definition of hairpin turns, our car stitching the snowy landscape to and fro, back and forth. With nearly every turn we saw signs indicating that we were entering a new county. Jefferson. Boulder. Gilpin. Then the reverse order.

We cracked up at the absurdity of the situation. We were seemingly going in circles, like so many humans, with no GPS. But we arrived at the bar, an ancient barn that had been converted to a business.

The bar downstairs was nearly empty, which seemed odd since there were lots of cars in the lot. Upstairs, said the bartender—that's where the action is.

We had a couple beers and listened to a surprisingly good, enigmatic band, replete with horns and acoustic guitars. Precisely at midnight, multicolored lights began flashing and bar workers passed out hula hoops to anyone who wanted one. I did. Matt did, too.

As the band played a fast one, we hula-hooped with strangers there at the backwoods bar on a snowy night in the mysterious mountains of Colorado.

Four

Shawn Randall Channeling Torah

Afew days before our interview with the fourth channeler, I received some distressing news: A buddy of
mine had committed suicide. We weren't the very clos-
est of friends—we played softball together and social-
ized from time to time—but still this revelation sent me
reeling.

"Sam" left behind two small children and a solid
career. He seemed like a generally happy and fulfilled
man; he was generous and quick with a quip. In retro-
spect, though, he had given me clues to his true state of
mind. He was going through a painful divorce and spoke
of money problems. He had also revealed to me over
beers a couple of times that he sometimes felt that he
had "settled" and didn't fully pursue his latent dream of
being a sports broadcaster. He believed it was too late for
that now, even though he was not yet forty, and that his
life was "all dug in."

At the time, it just seemed like generic grumbling,
the sort you might hear from anyone on any bar stool on

Earth. So it knocked the air out of me when I heard he'd chosen a fistful of pills over another day on the planet.

I wondered if, even at my nadir, I ever would have actually taken that radical step. These were the thoughts pinging the inside walls of my skull as I met Matt on a suburban street in Woodland Hills in the San Fernando Valley, only a few miles from where we did the interview with Darryl and Bashar. It was the first week of the new year, sky gray as granite, rain drizzling.

Because of the unsettling news I'd received and the drab weather, I was a bit melancholic that day. I was, however, eager to meet Shawn Randall, who has been channeling a being named "Torah" since 1983, so I talked myself into a chipper mood. A former ballet dancer and actress, Shawn now teaches classes in the Los Angeles area on how to become a trance channel.

When she greeted us at her office door, Shawn was poised and warm. She was sixty-five, but, again, could easily have been a decade younger. There was something up with these channelers . . . every single one of them looked younger than their chronological age.

Matt, who had gotten the hang of these shoots, set up quickly, and we were off and running. As with the others, I first talked to Shawn before the spirit took over.

"I have been interested in the metaphysical my entire life, but the channeling really started for me back in the early '80s in a class where we were really studying making a trans-bridge, an inter-psychic bridge to other sources of intelligence," she said. "And so it started in the context of that class.

"I had a very strong sense that this is a direction my life was supposed to take. It has all felt very good and natural and aligned. So I worked with a psychologist, Dr. Margo Chandley. And she would help me practice going into trance and let the entities talk. And it felt very natural to me, all the way along because I was always having the reassurance from my telepathic connection with my unseen friends that everything was going along as scheduled.

"And then I would get updates and recommendations from them, and things I could do to prepare. And it all felt really, really comfortable and very, very aligned. Very, very nice. Plus I had this wonderful psychologist who I could talk with about it and debrief about it. So I never felt odd or unusual. I know that some people have had it be very strange and unsettling. And it was never that way for me at all."

Shawn did not offer much in the way of describing Torah except as a "nonphysical friend. He describes himself as a 'multidimensional consciousness no longer choosing to incarnate.' The name itself, 'Torah,' means 'teaching of love and light,' and he has said it's not a direct or specific reference to Hebrew texts. So that's good enough for me."

And me. We were ready to get down to the channeling, so Shawn, as the others had done, closed her eyes and took those very deep breaths. She rolled her shoulders slightly, shook her arms. Only a few seconds later, her face was alight with wattage, a huge smile dominating her face as Torah shone through.

"Alright. Alright, we say greetings and greetings indeed to all of you and each of you, yes," said Torah. This voice was different and, as with Wendy when she went into trance state, seemed slightly British, though not as pronounced. "A pleasure to be with you in this way, very much a delight and pleasure to be speaking with you. You will have to direct us and begin in that way with your purpose for being here and your questions. So, dear ones, we would say welcome, and how would you like to begin today?"

As we went on, I found Torah's energy less bombastic than Bashar's, and perhaps closer to the gentleness of the Pleiadians. I could feel a breezy love essence emanating from Torah, and it made for a comfortable, relaxed interview. Given my somewhat fragile mental state, it was exactly what I needed.

≋

Q: Do you consider this a special time on Earth and, if it is, why?

A: We would simply categorize it as a special time because the evolution of human consciousness is becoming visible. Certainly it is becoming more mandatory. But it is becoming visible and it is becoming known, and it is becoming active and a part of life itself.

Q: Some people have called this an ascension process. Do you subscribe to that view, and if you do, what is ascension?

A: Well, we don't prefer to use the word "ascension" because it certainly has some Biblical overtones and harkens back to some old assumptions. And it carries a lot of baggage, that word, for our purposes. So we don't use that word. We can't speak for others, but perhaps they are speaking of an upliftment of vibration or frequency that is happening, and in that way we would say that human beings are certainly transforming. So that might be a word that we would use—transforming, or integrating, or individuating. This would be more in alignment with the way we talk.

So if you look at transforming, well, that is happening and the transformation of consciousness on the planet is not something that simply goes from A to Z and is done in a certain amount of time period and by the date of such and such and so and so, bingo, it's going to be done. No, no. It is like the changes of the ages. It takes a long time. One can't say the exact date when the Aquarian Age began, for example, or when it finishes, for example—only approximations. And so it is with the idea of evolution and transformation of human consciousness that this is something that is protracted; it is over a period of time without an actual beginning. Now, human beings tend to like dates. They love dates. Because it gives them a sense of order, a sense of placement. It's like what's termed your "Harmonic Convergence," 1987, etcetera. These dates become milestones to people, and they can say that is when something happened; you graduated college in that year or got married or whatever it might be. And it gives an order to how people think of things, certainly so. So that is coming about these days as people are enjoying giving themselves an order.

They're giving themselves a deadline, actually, with the 2012 coming in the future. "Ah yes, by 2012, this and such and so and so." In that regard it's like a deadline people are giving themselves in consciousness. "We better have it together by 2012 or something terrible might happen." And of course it won't be that way. The date isn't suddenly, instantly going to change the whole planet. So it's a special time and yet it's human beings who make it special. It's the focus of the intention and attention that the human beings place on certain dates and certain time periods that indeed invest them with what they are to become. And so yes, it is a great time of transformation and upliftment, certainly so, a very exciting time, and it is also a very important time to try to bring the new wisdom, which is the old wisdom, by the way, but to bring the new wisdom forward in a way that can be of practical use on the planet.

Let it go into your lives, let it go into what you wish to do for the planet, for the ecology, for the political systems, etcetera. It's a time of integrating, not separating. Integrating one's integrity, one's principles, one's ideals with how one lives one's life and how one creates the planet to be in higher order.

Q: So it's not time to be meditating alone on a mountaintop. You really have to get out and live life, and embody some of these principles.

A: Absolutely it's time to embody these principles; it's time to live them. It's a time to put your walk and your talk where your mind is. Really, really a time to live it and be it, and put good intentions into action. Certainly.

Q: So there truly is no real significance to the year 2012, even though many people are focused on that?

A: Oh, there's a lot of significance astronomically and astrologically. Certainly so. There's a lot of significance, but it's up for a lot of interpretation, as was the Harmonic Convergence, for example. You could use it however you wished, and it is a wonderful opportunity for a marker for a progression of human consciousness to become more visible.

Q: You refer to yourself as "we" rather than "I." Could you talk about that?

A: Certainly so. We are aware of ourselves on many, many, many levels of being in consciousness, and the aspect of ourselves that we are aware of as we speak to you through this channel is very different than aspects of ourselves we are aware of in our own dimensional reality. Because there are so many, in that sense, levels of our capital "S" self, we feel that the pronoun "I" doesn't quite cover it. So we say "we."

≋

I found myself not quite as engaged in this exchange as I had been with the previous three. My mind kept pulsing back to my friend . . . I saw him catching a softball in left field, firing it into me at shortstop. I now realize I certainly could have asked Torah about his suicide, but it somehow felt inappropriate, too personal. So I went with something more universal . . .

≋

Q: What is your take on the Law of Attraction?

A: The Law of Attraction is very important and dynamic. It's an ordering principle of the universe. It's been around for a long, long time. It's always been there, actually. And the Law of Attraction basically talks about the law of affinity, like attracting like. The tricky thing about the Law of Attraction is that it must be viewed for its complexity. Oversimplifying it leads one perhaps into even delusion. You must see it in the larger light. Just as we spoke a moment ago of being aware of ourselves at many levels of consciousness, so it is that human beings have many levels of consciousness. The conscious, the unconscious, the subconscious mind. The collective unconscious participation and the higher conscious mind. And if all those levels are not aligned in a certain way, then indeed the Law of Attraction won't work.

So you can think with your conscious mind one way, and say to yourself all day long "I know I'm deserving, I know I'm deserving, abundance is coming to me, abundance is coming to me."

But if the subconscious and unconscious are not on board with that, not lined up with it, then you're not going to be able to work that Law of Attraction. You will be attracting from the other level of consciousness. So the Law of Attraction has been oversimplified, and we would suggest that it's far more intricate than it's often made out to be in its more popular version these days. So we always say to people, "okay, Law of Attraction, it's a wonderful thing, but go deeper, look farther, understand the complexity of what frequency is all about. Understand the complexity of your own consciousness and your subconscious agendas, your subconscious beliefs. Understand them and if some of them need changing, set about to change them."

> So you can . . . say to yourself all day long "I know I'm deserving . . . abundance is coming to me" . . . (b)ut if the subconscious and unconscious are not on board with that . . . you're not going to be able to work that Law of Attraction.

Q: How best to do that? Sometimes it's difficult to get to the root belief.

A: Yes indeed. You do that by having contact with meditative states of mind. Being able to have a rapport, a working rapport, with one's subconscious mind is very important. Having a working rapport with the unconscious mind is deeper still and even trickier. But that rapport with subconscious and unconscious can be achieved by really paying close attention to one's dreams, the way one affects visualization, and guided imagery, for example. Affecting change at that level of guided imagery can be very, very helpful. Also monitoring thoughts and feelings and really choosing to change the blockages that are there in thoughts and feelings. Some people who say they want to be happy, for example, are instead more invested in being angry or righteous. So if they monitor that and they are able to say, "gee, look at that, my actions say I'm more invested in being angry and righteous, therefore let me really set out to change that in my thoughts and feelings, in my actions," it meditatively works.

Also you can do some effective change with behavior modification. Because if you modify and behave with certain disciplines, sooner or later your subconscious gets the idea. "Ah, they're serious, they really do want to believe they're deserving. They really are choosing to believe that. These actions are showing." The subconscious responds to consistent change of actions. So we say you can change from the outside in, and from the inside out. It's best done if both are put into place. We like to think of it as burning the candle at both ends. Then the fire comes together at the center and bingo, you've got change in the being and the vibration of the person.

≡

I wondered to myself whether channeled material would have helped my buddy cope. Could he have used it to assist in raising his own vibration, thus attracting more of what he wanted, more light, more positivity? I recalled that I had mentioned my interest in channeling to him a few times, but he was disinterested at best, so eventually I just dropped it. I tried to keep my head in the interview by sticking to an established list of questions.

⬯

Q: Dreams often seem to be visual gibberish. How can a person better interpret dreams?

A: Well, the first thing to do is write them down. A very simple way of working with dreams is to write them down and circle the phrases and words that stand out to you, that hit you in the gut, so to speak. And then look to see: what does that remind you of, something in the past, something that may have happened to you? What is the significance? Dreams are really there to teach, and in many, many ways they do teach. Big subject, dreams. Wonderful subject, dreams. Because dreams are a way that people touch the nonlocal state of their being every day. Every day you get to touch your non-local self through your dream state. Outside linear time, outside space and time, you get to have dreams every day and write about them, remember what they felt like, remember what you learned from them.

Flying dreams—oh, what wonderful things. Flying dreams are important because they are teaching you what it's like to have total free will, total free choice. They are reminding you what it's like between your lifetimes. The freedom, the dominion, the wonderful wonder of awareness and how there are no limitations brought by the physical realm.

⬯

I realized I was still distracted by thoughts of Sam and forced myself to keep my focus. I just couldn't shake the notion of someone I knew actually choosing such a sudden physical end for himself. It struck me that it's so difficult to really know what's swirling inside another human. He had lots of problems, but the entities all say it's one's *thoughts* about those problems that are paramount—not the challenges themselves.

≡

Q: There's also a lot of talk about how "thought creates." I think it does, but is it more complicated than that?

A: Very complicated. Thought creates, but you have to look at which thought is creating. As we mentioned, the subconscious has its own agendas, and you're not always conscious of its thoughts. So conscious thought is very significant here and subconscious or unconscious thought is still existing; it's like a frequency that's always being emitted. So if one can become aligned with the sense of one's subconscious, then your conscious thought is more likely to manifest or create what it wants.

Q: A lot of humans desire more abundance in their lives, yet don't seem able to produce it. What's some practical advice about creating more abundance in life?

A: Well, first you want to look at the history and the conditioning of the person. The person is conditioned for some degree of abundance or non-abundance, depending on the preexisting conditions with the parents growing up. And so conditioning is the first place to look—because the conditioning will determine what the belief systems are and what the subconscious is holding on to. If there's limitation there, then you want to sort of address that therapeutically, transformationally, to heal whatever that misconception is, because all humans are deserving, innately, inherently deserving. It's a matter of recognizing it, owning it, understanding it, and believing it.

≣

I wondered if Sam had that sense of *deserving* the life he wanted, deserving true joy and fulfillment. The answer, I concluded, was self-evident, considering what he'd just done.

Did I feel deserving of abundance in all things? Maybe not totally, no. But unlike my dead friend, I was willing to keep working on it.

≣

Q: Are there specific modalities or techniques that will help a person produce more abundance or change the core belief system to produce more abundance?

A: Ah, well said. Change the core belief system and all the tributaries of that core belief system. There are many, many ways. Again, we say start by healing the former conditioning that is there. Working in altered states is very significant, because in altered states of consciousness the conscious, subconscious, and unconscious can dialogue with each other—and the intention that you have consciously can be absorbed into the unconscious. Affirmations are very nice in that way. As you consciously repeat affirmations and feel them with your body, remember that the subconscious aligns with the feelings in the body. And if you're really feeling the excitement and the fun of "I'm feeling my abundance and I'm wanting to believe it and I'm changing my conditioning, I'm feeling it very fully," the subconscious with enough repetition starts to get the idea. "Oh, he's serious. Oh, she's serious. She really feels it now. I better consider changing that belief structure there." So affirmations can work that way, changing the energy that one is feeling around, feeling very fully with the body, working with the synapses of the brain. Absolutely so. Work with the synapses of the brain. Send those neurons down different roads, you know. And over and over repetition of such things can produce change as well.

Basically when we talk about changing a person's abundance situation, it almost needs to be taken on a case-by-case basis, because human beings are so different. But by and large there are certain things that can work very well. One is the idea of changing your thoughts, changing your feelings, and working fully with affirmations.

≡

I still felt it was somehow inappropriate to get into specifics, but thoughts of Sam kept drumming my brain so I finally addressed the topic, if obliquely.

≡

Q: There seem to be many people—not everyone, but many people—in despair. Why is that and what can they do to get out of it?

A: We would say perhaps another way to address the subject you're talking about is to say that "it seems like we are living in troubled times." But different people will respond to that differently. Some people will not take that with despair, or to their despair. Some people will choose the optimistic high road and stay very proactive in making change. Other people may say, "oh, these are troubled times, it's too much for me, I'm going to acquiesce and just be at the mercy of these times rather than being a chooser and a proactive change instrument."

So if people are feeling despairing, then perhaps that is their individual road— some might call it karma, or what they are to learn to transform. Because the world itself right now isn't in despair, but there are some troubled times in this world. New problems, ideological conflicts, different kinds of warfare or thoughts and ideals and principles. And in that way a lot of change is on the planet. But it isn't in and of itself something that would produce despair. It's the person that allows despair.

≋

Yes, that's what he had done. Succumbed to it, didn't proactively choose differently, consistently, moment-by-moment and day-by-day. I realized that's how I had pulled myself out of the quicksand of despondency . . . not in one giant motion or a single transcendent epiphany, but inch by hard-won inch.

≋

Q: What is your opinion of humanity in general?

A: Well, at this particular time we view humans, and we very much enjoy viewing humans, as great potential starting to realize itself in the face of ever-increasing challenges. The challenges can be daunting, and yet the human capacity for infinite possibilities is truly on the horizon more than ever before. That is because capacities in consciousness have expanded and grown. People are aware of the many levels of consciousness, that altered states of consciousness are available to all people. Everyone has dreams, for example. That's an altered state of consciousness.

So we say that humanity is in a very exciting process of

bringing potential and possibility to the forefront. And yes, it is coming in the context of having to meet the challenges of strange conflicts that no one could have ever anticipated, the conflicts that are happening against the backdrop of religious holy wars and these concepts that have to be wrestled with. You take some of the very basic things you see in everyday life and you look at what's at the top of that pyramid that it's coming down from? It may appear to you as, "well can't fly out of LAX today, because of a color-coded warning." It's coming from this greater challenge that humanity is faced with at this time. And fortunately there are people who are looking at those greater challenges. People who are connecting with higher principles and spiritual truths through channeling or other forms of enlightened inspiration and finding answers to some of these large questions. So it's a very exciting time for people, very challenging, and it certainly is a wake-up call, isn't it.

Q: Is it true that the outside reflects the inside?

A: Absolutely so. "Let there be peace on Earth and let it begin with me." That wonderful old adage could never be truer. The more one is in peace and harmony with oneself, the more one can be in peace and harmony with one's environment, one's family, one's country, and one's planet. As well as one's planetary ecology and the forces of nature.

Q: How will life differ for us within ten or twenty years?

A: Well, one thing you can expect is a great deal more awareness and self-responsibility. Let's look at the metaphor right now that you're seeing with ecology. There's been an ecological crisis for fifteen or twenty years, but only now are people becoming aware of it. And people are starting to slowly change their habits, and different sources of energy are being explored and developed. It's always been there, but now people are more actively participating to make the changes. So take that little analogy and switch it over to the bigger issues. Ideological differences, fundamentalism, the misunderstandings between cultures. The culture of commercialism versus cultures that are more ritual- or action-based. And as more people become aware, as they are now ecologically, and it becomes part of the speech, part of the way people communicate, part of understanding, we would say a tipping point can be reached. The tipping point has to do with the collective consciousness or the consensus reality. So what you're going to see in the future is a collective consciousness that is slowly expanding to a greater level of self-responsibility, psychologically and spiritually. Being responsible for one's anger, for one's fears. Being responsible for the impact one has on other human beings. That is so important, and you will see more of that behaviorally.

Now, when people ask us what changes there might be in ten or twenty years, they are thinking of outer world changes, context. We are talking about *content*. The content of consciousness is going to be more aware of itself, more articulate, more forthcoming, a part of a collective consciousness change, and the tipping point hasn't been reached yet. When does that collective consciousness come into its fullness, when will that tipping point be? A lot of people feel that's what 2012 is about, but we would say consciousness is going to determine that tipping point. How many aware people on the planet is it going to take that are able to put their awareness into their speech and into their actions before the collective consensus is affected? And that is yet to be determined; no one knows exactly when and how it'll happen.

But you will see in the next ten or twenty years a change

in verbiage as people are able to articulate more about self-responsibility. Already seeing that. As people are able to articulate more about other levels of consciousness, higher consciousness—you're already seeing some of that. People talk about "my higher self, my higher consciousness, my higher power," different terms. And then behaving from that level of integrity is what you will begin to see as well, eventually.

> *How many aware people on the planet is it going to take that are able to put their awareness into their speech and into their actions before the collective consensus is affected?*

≡

I wondered if Sam, now in spirit, had regrets about exiting flesh. Or was he now truly in a place where all judgment and guilt simply evaporated like dew in the morning sun? It struck me that he certainly must not have felt empowered on Earth; in fact he must have been prostrate with an extreme sense of powerlessness.

≡

Q: What do you say to people who are not feeling empowered? How can they feel more empowered?

A: We would suggest that if people are not feeling empowered, the first thing we do is remind them that they are telling themselves some lies. Fear is usually under all loss of power. You lose power because there is something you fear. Remember that F.E.A.R. is "false evidence appearing real." A lot of people are aware of that now. "I'm believing this story, I'm telling myself that I'm powerless." So when people say, "I know I'm powerless" or "I'm feeling powerless," we say, "ah, that's a story you're telling yourself. That's a story you're telling yourself based on fear." So it's so important to start waking up to the truth of one's own nature. The truth of one's own nature is what one finds when you go within and discover the connection to all and to God/Goddess, All That Is, that lies deep at the heart of the true self.

Q: How do you define God?

A: People project humanity onto God, yes? And the religions have done this in order to help people conceive God, and it certainly makes some sense. If you've got to have something to sink your teeth into, something to imagine as an image of God, then if that's what you need, then you need a "religion"—an organization, a code if you will, a codification of what God is into a personification. And in history that's what's happened. People have had to project some kind of personification onto All That Is in order to conceptualize it.

Now there's a shift. We would suggest there's a new myth of God arising at this time. And that is a very exciting prospect, to take the idea of God into a larger context of God/Goddess, All That Is. That God is not simply a masculine image, per se, but is a principle that is masculine, feminine, and the synergy of both. So this new myth of God in that regard, seeing that God/Goddess is creation itself, is consciousness itself, involves underlying ordering principles of anything you can think and feel and know as a human being, and even the things you cannot think, feel, and know as a human being, is All That Is. That new myth of God can keep one moving forward into new discoveries of these luminous, numinous, transcendent operating principles that keep the universe going. That keep consciousness itself, which is the universe, expanding and growing.

It's very important to see that God/Goddess, All That Is, cannot be defined in terms, in words. It must be known experientially.

Q: So even you don't know God fully?

A: No, no, absolutely not. And if we did, we wouldn't exist. In that way there is not one consciousness that can know God/Goddess fully. You can know what you know, you can know what you are capable of knowing, but there's always more. All That Is and life itself is consciousness, and at the highest octave it is love. Not the human romantic love that you think of. There is a form of transcendent transpersonal love that at the highest octave is All That Is, is *all* there is.

Q: When we don't have earthly bodies—I assume we're more fully aware at that point—why do we decide to come into bodies and take on this cloak of amnesia?

A: To learn more about yourself, to gain greater dominion, greater skill of consciousness, to live the creative principle itself. Because when you come into a physical existence, you become a creator in the physical dimension. You're creating your life and the activities, your experiences, your responses to the experiences. But it's all about the progression of the evolution of one's soul. And reincarnating allows you more and more understanding and knowledge through experience.

Q: Many humans think of Jesus Christ as a savior; why do people think that way?

A: Well, it goes back to what we were saying before. Many people need the personification in order to be able to identify with the idea that they are also divine, that the kingdom of heaven is within. And if Jesus is an image of that, is a role model for that, is an excellent example of that, then people can aspire to it. It's something that people need, that idea that "I can be saved," that idea. And then hopefully one gets to the understanding, as Jesus taught, that no, it's *you* that is going to save yourself. It lies within you. Jesus was the bearer of that message, but the message and its energy must be discovered within one's own individual self.

So Jesus as a consciousness, absolutely a master. Many of his teachings are misunderstood; indeed, the resurrection was to teach about immortal life, not that one must suffer. The archetype of Jesus the savior is still very powerful on the planet, and yet that slowly is being replaced by the Aquarian Age, which is shifting the emphasis for people finding it within themselves, instead of needing it to be out there as a figure.

Q: In a sense, do you think some people are afraid of how powerful they truly are?

A: Yes, that's true because a lot of people are afraid of their own anger and fear and they can feel how powerful that is. And if they were to ever unleash their true power, they would also potentially unleash their anger and their fear. And of course that's not what real power is. Real power is the ability to act from an integrated, self-aware place of personal dominion.

≣

Something Sam didn't have, and that I was still working on. I realized that we try to take shortcuts to this state of being. I know I certainly have at times—through excessive drinking and, looking back, I recognized Sam did as well.

≣

Q: On Earth many people overuse drugs and alcohol, and it's like they're trying to fill a hole in themselves. What is that hole?

A: The hole is a feeling of being disconnected and disenfranchised in some way from one's life. We talk about an archetype called "separation." At the deepest level in the human psyche there is this archetype called separation, and it's based on the fact that you separate yourself from source when you choose to become born. And everyone has that experience over and over; every lifetime you choose to be incarnated you experience separation. Separation from source, separation from unconditional love, separation from the light, separation, separation. And so that can become like the hole. "I feel disconnected, I feel separated, something's missing in my life." The desire for something transcendent becomes very, very strong.

And instead of seeking it authentically through one's spirituality, people will often seek it through external substances and mind-altering substances. We would suggest that they're seeking it in the wrong place, but it is an authentic hunger for knowing one's own divine nature, for experiencing one's divine nature. That true hunger can lead you into great discovery and great freedom. It isn't restriction. There's a big misunderstanding in society in many cultures that if you're going to become "spiritual," you're going to get real restricted—and that's because of the old dogmas of different religions, different churches, and different ways. But spirituality itself is not at all restricting in one's way of experiencing life.

Q: So as you go along you'll tend to feel more and more freedom?

A: Absolutely. When one is connected with source, there's

no sense of the separation. One is in the flow of that abundance, the flow of love, the flow of joy, the flow of creation.

Q: Is it true that our entire being is not focused in this body?

A: Yes, you are a multidimensional being and all your dimensions are not incarnated into this body called you. It's true that your entire consciousness is not defined inside the limits of your skin. Your skin isn't wrapped around your consciousness. You are multidimensional consciousness, and the more people explore that, the more unlimited they feel; the more connected they feel with source. When people are having mental telepathy, they know there's more to them than meets the eye because they can feel it; they've had telepathy with someone else. So when one thinks of having telepathy with other sources of intelligence or nonphysical sources of intelligence, that's very expanding. And to have telepathy with one's own higher consciousness, to have that sense of self-understanding, is going to evolve you. So you can't be all incorporated into one body because you are part of a sea of consciousness.

Q: I'm still confused about how we can be having different experiences and different lives simultaneously.

A: We'd like you to consider this metaphor that we like to use for understanding simultaneity and chronology at the same time. In other words, simultaneous lives and chronological lives are a total paradox, but here's how one can begin to understand it. Imagine a jar of jelly beans. And they're all different colors, there's green ones and yellow ones and red ones and blue ones. Let's just pretend that those jelly beans are your lifetimes. And there they are all together. How could they possibly be chronological? Well, imagine that if you were to take off the top and pick up a jelly bean and discover that it is connected to another jelly bean by a string. So that you could pull out a string of jelly beans and hold it like that, like a necklace of pearls. Here you have chronological lifetimes; there they are one after the other in the reality of space and time.

So it depends on how you're looking at the jelly beans. How you are wanting to experience the jelly beans. So imagine there you are, you've got your jelly beans in the jar, you, your higher self, your soul, and some very wise elders on the other side get together and say "hmm, which jelly bean are we going to shine a light on? Where are we going to focus now?"

Q: Really well-explained. Thanks. What is a lightworker?

A: What that means is that they choose to bring awareness to the things that they do, they choose to shine a light, show deeper meaning, deeper content, a deeper purpose to things. Enlighten things, lighten things up and even bring a little humor into it. One could say you're a lightworker if you're Don Rickles in Las Vegas. That's quite a unique interpretation of a lightworker, but people can be lightworkers in many, many different ways. It's about intention. "What am I intending to do? I want to enlighten, I want to bring light, I want to help open people's eyes, I want to put my efforts and endeavors toward assisting individuals." Such people would be lightworkers.

> You live in a reality of polarity and duality, but there's something that's stronger than that, and that is the non-duality of existence itself.

Q: What about the dark? Is it necessary?

A: In the reality of polarity and duality, yes it is. You live in a reality of polarity and duality, but there's something that's stronger than that, and that is the non-duality of existence itself. In the human existence, there is light and dark, there is contrast, there are opposites. There is polarity and duality.

Q: Is it good advice if you want a happy and fulfilled life to choose the light?

A: Well, of course. Absolutely. And also to have a balance of awareness of both. One doesn't want to be in the light by being in the denial of one's shadow. One wants to be conscious of being enlightened or light because one is willing to work with one's shadow. Like Buddha, who used his meditation and disciplines and practices in that way. Those disciplines and practices would be about integrating one's dark side. Overcoming one's challenges of the limited self, getting past the illusions of separation.

Q: In wrapping up, is there anything you'd like to leave us with, advice or uplifting words or anything you'd like to add?

A: There's a great sage who likes to say, "if you want enlightenment, lighten up." And certainly so, it is absolutely true. We would suggest that one of the great secrets to lightening up is being willing to heal and transform one's angers and fears so that the joys can be fuller and richer, and so that creation can become a very active principle in your life very consciously. What would we like to leave people with? Well, we wouldn't want to leave people. We would like to say it is a joy and pleasure, a great, great joy to interact with people because we see people in ways they do not see themselves, and it is beautiful. We see you in ways you do not see yourself, and it is magnificent.

And for that it is a source of great gratitude to us that we are able to come and to interact and to do our best to shine some light on the true nature of the divine self that lies at the heart of each individual. So it is we will at this time depart, and we send you all much love, as we always do. Feeling it deeply, richly. Much, much love.

Q: Thank you.

≋

Shawn came out of trance and, like the others, took a moment to recover and get grounded. I asked how she felt after channeling.

"Just wonderful," she said. "It's such a gift. It allows me access to lighter frequencies and such loving energies. I always feel very good, very alive when I come back into body."

Outside, the sky was pelting us with hard, wet rivulets, so Matt and I didn't stick around for a post-channel discussion. My mind was still on Sam, but the talk with Torah had helped. As I drove home through the rain, my clothes were damp, but inside I felt warm and dry.

Five

John Cali Channeling
Chief Joseph

Over the next week, I had a chance to more fully process the Sam situation. I concluded that his solution to the vagaries of earthly life was indeed drastic, but from my limited perspective I couldn't really judge it. Yes, his family and friends would have a lot to deal with due to his decision . . . but this wasn't a "bad" thing, since there is no death. It's all just life everlasting, whether in human form or another. He sought relief from a life he perceived to be strangling him, and he received it. Maybe his passing was just the sort of catalyst some people in his orbit might need to begin waking up. The jarring event that some seem to require, as Tobias had suggested. Now Sam was off on a new adventure in some other realm, and I felt sure we would rendezvous again at some point.

So when Matt and I embarked on our trip to Wyoming, I was feeling happy and energized. We flew from

LAX to Denver, and then took a regional puddle jumper to Cody, Wyoming.

When we landed at the small Cody airport around 9 PM, it was all but closed up. The pink-cheeked woman at the Hertz counter had stayed open that late only because we'd booked ahead and she knew we were coming.

You might say there was a nip in the air—it was 12 degrees—but this time I had no complaints as we drove the rental to our luxurious lodgings—a Motel 6 on the edge of this ten-thousand-person red state town. I was viewing this entire trip as an adventure, and I was excited about who we'd come to see—so what was a little chill? Especially for a guy who grew up in the face-numbing, phalange-freezing winters of Minnesota.

The man we were to interview was John Cali, who has been publicly channeling Chief Joseph, former chief of the Nez Perce Indians, since 1995. I had made contact with John a couple years earlier and had had a channeled session by phone with Chief Joseph. Some of the insights he offered into my own life had truly struck a chord, so when I decided to make the film, I knew John and the former chief had to be part of it.

John said he'd "downsized" in the past few years and was living in a small place, so he nixed the idea of shooting at his abode. The Motel 6 rooms are far from spacious themselves, so I asked the hotel manager if we could shoot for a couple hours in one of their suites. He graciously agreed and didn't even charge us extra.

When John knocked on the suite door the next morning, we were all set up and ready to roll. He was dressed in jeans and cowboy boots, and looked as fit as a young boxer. I asked him about how he kept in such good shape, and he told me that he ran about three miles nearly every day, hiked, and lifted weights. Matt and I were both shocked when he told us his age: seventy. I'd pegged him as perhaps mid-fifties, and Matt remarked that he looked about twenty years younger than his seventy years. So, again, rather than Botox to keep that youthful appearance, I might suggest that one take up channeling.

John revealed he'd never been interviewed in front of a camera before and admitted to being slightly nervous. He seemed somewhat shy and reserved by nature anyway, so I was inwardly concerned that he might freeze up.

But when we turned on the lights and cameras, John melted into the interview as easily as rainwater running down a roof.

"What really started me on the path of channeling was reading the book *Opening to Channel* by Sanaya Roman and Duane Packer," said John. "I read the book several times and followed their procedures, and the end result of that was that a spirit guide came to me. She appeared to me—this was in 1986—as an American Indian woman, and her name was Tamara. And so I channeled her for a few years. I was aware, sort of on the periphery of my awareness, of this male Indian. I didn't know who he was. I didn't know if he was real or if it was my imagination or where he was coming from. I didn't really trust myself as a channel then. And so it was kind of a scary process for me in the beginning, and I didn't have a lot of confidence in myself. But I knew there was something there that was beyond me."

So, I asked, how did it develop further?

"Well," John went on, "in 1992, I was experiencing some pretty hefty challenges in my personal and spiritual life.

Chief Joseph began speaking to me, and I knew who he was because, as I said, he'd been sort of lingering about on the periphery for six years. He offered to help me. I said, 'Sure, I can use all the help I can get!'

"And so it began. Joseph and I continued like that, one-on-one, for several years. We dealt mostly with my personal issues. We also worked privately with a small circle of close friends. But we did nothing publicly.

"Then, toward the end of 1995, Joseph asked if I'd consider channeling publicly for others, especially since it had been so helpful to me. I said, 'No, I don't think so.' But one thing led to another. And, ultimately, Joseph prevailed. So we started doing private sessions for others outside my small circle.

"When I first started communicating with Joseph, I was a real novice at that sort of thing. And I was sometimes uneasy when I channeled him.

"But as I became more comfortable in my own abilities and in the abilities of spirit, my powers of communication, of channeling, became greater. The more I channeled Joseph, the more I discovered I was able to access the higher aspects of this entity I'd known as Chief Joseph. I was able to reach into what you might call the 'Joseph soul group,' a group of spirits who are clearly a highly evolved and powerful family of teachers."

I asked John why he'd initially told Joseph he didn't want to go public, and if he had any regrets about acceding to the "dead" Indian's wishes.

"I grew up in a Roman Catholic family of Sicilian immigrants, so this sort of thing was simply nothing none of us had ever been interested in, much less actually done," he said. "So I guess there was just natural hesitation there on my part. Most of my family, even today, after I've been channeling Joseph for fifteen years, doesn't know what I do. They have some idea. 'Cause I don't talk about it to them, and they don't ask me. They know I do something 'weird.'"

"So let the weirdness begin!" I exclaimed. "Let's do a bit of channeling."

John settled comfortably into his chair, took a sip of water, and closed his eyes. There were no tics or body reactions of any kind; he didn't even breathe deeply, as the others had.

A few seconds later, a voice unaltered from John's own said, "May the Great Spirit be with you always." Chief Joseph had joined us. Not only was John's transition into trance seamless, but he also sometimes opened his eyes, unlike any of the others. Every word seemed dipped in goodwill, and the resultant energy in the room was akin to fluffy sheep's wool.

≡

Q: We're thrilled to be here, Chief Joseph—thank you for coming. Is there anything you'd like to open with or talk about as an opening statement?

A: We have as our goal in this work we're doing with John and with the others whose lives we touch to simply help people live a more joyful, abundant life. And whatever it takes to achieve that, we're willing to do. So that in a nutshell, if you will, is our work.

Q: What are the basics for people to do that?

A: The real base basic, if you will, is to simply remember who you are and why you're here. You are spirit, you are God. You are all God, and once you can integrate that into your being, your human mind, then you'll find your lives becoming much easier and more joyful and more abundant. But what often happens to people is they get caught up in the world around them, and it's easy for that to happen because there's so much out there that's flooding you. If you pay a lot of attention to your mainstream news media, you're probably going to be depressed a good part of the time. You're probably going to be sad and upset. If you pay a lot of attention to the bad stuff in the world today, you're not going to feel joyful. But there's far more good stuff out there today than there is bad stuff.

Part of the problem is the mainstream news media's focus on the bad stuff—they suck people in, if you will. And your governments are very disempowering to the individual. So you have so many forces working against self-empowerment and against reclaiming your power that it can be hard for people who are not yet spiritually aware or *as* spiritually aware as more and more people are becoming today. It's particularly hard for those people to stand up to the modern world's influence.

Q: What are some ways people can become more self-empowered?

A: Well, you certainly have to get in touch with yourself. One of the best ways of doing that in our view is by meditation, whatever that means to you. It can be something as simple as taking a few moments each day and getting yourself into a comfortable place on a chair or even lying on a bed and focusing on your breathing. And that centers you, it gets you in touch with your body, and it also opens you up to the world of spirit in a way that most people are not open in their normal waking consciousness each day. Certainly it's never beneficial to anyone to do anything that does not feel good to them. And so many humans are doing things that don't feel good to them.

The perfect example of that is people are often in jobs they hate. They're doing the work for the money, not because they love it, and that is very counterproductive to what people want for themselves. So anytime you're doing anything that does not feel good to you, or that does not resonate with you—even if it is a job that's paying you thousands, and hundreds of thousands of dollars—if it's something you really dislike, you're doing yourself a great disservice and you're distancing yourself more and more from your higher self. You can't disconnect from your higher self, but you can certainly get out of alignment from your higher self, and that's what's happening with so many people today.

So the basic goal here is to get back into alignment with your higher self, and once you do that, you'll be flooded, you'll be inundated with the joy that your higher self feels in every present moment. Your higher self exists in a state of perfect bliss, joy, and ecstasy. And your goal as a human extension of this higher self is to get more in touch with that higher, divine part of you.

Q: Is it too simplistic to say that most choices are choices between fear and love?

A: No, we think that's quite accurate. Fear is rampant on your planet today. And it's so easy to get sucked into that. The opposite of fear is love, appreciation, joy. We define love as the choice to see the divinity in all beings, not just human beings, not just spirit beings, but *all* beings: All That Is. Everything that exists, even that rocky hillside outside your window there, everything that exists has a divine aspect. It is part of what you call God, or Goddess. So once you can shift your normal human consciousness and be willing with conscious effort to acknowledge that God really is All That Is and that you are a part of God, you are God, and begin to look for those divine aspects in your everyday lives—people you meet on the street, family members, loved ones, friends, dogs, animals certainly, grizzly bears, rattlesnakes—they're all divine. If you can see that divine spark that exists in everything that exists, then you will begin to see as your higher self sees. You'll begin to see as God sees. As God sees you, as God sees the Earth, as God sees all creatures on the Earth. Everything that makes up the Earth. As God sees God.

The opposite of all of that is fear. You can only feel fear when you forget who you are, when you lose sight of God. When you lose sight of who everyone around you is, of what everything around you is. God is everywhere, God is good, God is love. Fear has no place in that. It cannot. You can't have fear and love existing in the same place, if you will.

Q: Sometimes it's hard not to go into fear. For instance, a person is out of money, has mouths to feed, whatever. What do they do then?

A: We would never advocate that someone who is in fear deny it. Admit that you have the fear. It's okay. You don't have to beat yourself over the head because you're afraid, or because you're sad, or because you're grieving. But it's also just as important to know that whenever you're in a situation like that, whether it's grief or sadness or fear, doesn't matter what it is, that there is a way out of it. If you're absolutely terrified, reach for a thought that's a little bit better than that. Maybe instead of being absolutely terrified you can move up

> *We define love as the choice to see the divinity in all beings, not just human beings, not just spirit beings, but all beings: All That Is.*

the scale a bit to being terribly afraid. And then you can move up from that to being just a little bit fearful, and so on up the scale. When somebody's enmeshed in some kind of deep negative emotion, it's always better to take it baby step by baby step rather than trying to make a quantum leap from fear to love in ten seconds or less.

Whenever you are in that state, know that you're not caught there. You're not going to be dragged down into doom and destruction because you're feeling what you're feeling at the moment. Know that your higher self or God or whatever divine power you believe in is there, pulling for you. You are never alone; there is always help out there no matter how far down you think you've fallen.

Q: For myself, I don't know why I do this, but when I feel I get to a very high vibration, I regress. Can you speak to that?

A: Certainly. There's an ebb and flow to everything, David. And so while you're in this human experience that you've chosen, this physical experience, there are going to be these ups and downs. And again, it's okay. Don't beat yourself over the head because you're high and then you're not so high. You're growing, you're expanding, you're evolving all the time and each high brings you to a point of growth that you've never achieved before. So you're growing and evolving and getting better and better and better. Know that in this up-and-down process, your overall situation is that you're growing. These cycles are helping you to grow—personally as a human being, and you're helping us in these dimensions of spirit to grow also, because we also are changing constantly, just like you are.

Q: How does that work?

A: Because you're a part of us, and we're a part of you. So

every positive thought you think, for example, ripples out into the world around you. To the physical world around you, but it also ripples out into the dimensions of spirit where we live. And so it's a give-and-take. We give to you, you give to us. We take from you, you take from us. It's a beautiful rhythm of life, if you will, that we see this as. It is a two-way street.

Q: Is it too simplistic to say "thought creates"? Is it more complex than that? Does it go beyond that?

A: No. Thought creates. What you're mostly thinking and feeling, you're manifesting. So if you're mostly thinking positive thoughts and feeling good feelings, then you're growing. If you mire yourself down with negative thoughts and the resultant negative feelings as many people do today, then that just drags you down. You do create with your thoughts. What you're thinking mostly is what you're going to manifest in your life.

Q: That ties in with the Law of Attraction?

A: Yes. Absolutely.

Q: How do you describe the Law of Attraction?

A: When you're thinking something—whether you consider it negative or positive, or God or the universe, however you want to word it—it matches that vibration that you're putting out. The Law of Attraction is very impersonal. It's not going to say, "Well Johnny's been a good boy today so we're going to reward him. Or Suzy's been a bad girl today so we're going to punish her." It's very impersonal; it has nothing to do with the concept of a punishing or judgmental God.

So whatever you're thinking, positive or negative, you're setting up a vibration around you. John has had recent experience with this in his family. Several people have been, recently, very ill, and eventually they died. They were always thinking, if you will, thoughts of bad health. Thinking themselves beyond the point of healing. They put out that vibration, the Law of Attraction matched it, and they moved on.

Q: So the Law of Attraction is like a perfect mirror, almost?

A: Yes. It's going to bring to you exactly what matches your vibration. Now we realize that people don't want to die of some painful illness or in a car accident or whatever, but every death, we have said several times over the years, every death is really a suicide. Because nothing can happen to you vibrationally that you're not a party to, if you will. In other words, if you're constantly afraid of dying in a car accident, you're probably going to die in a car accident. If you're constantly believing that your body, no matter what its condition, healthy or unhealthy, has the resources to bring itself back to a state of perfect health, you're going to achieve that state of perfect health. The Law of Attraction facilitates this on either end of the spectrum.

Q: Is it true that at some level, everyone chooses when to die?

A: Yes, we believe that. Probably the more dramatic examples of that are people who are terminally ill, so to speak, who refuse to go before, for example, a family member arrives who lives at a distance. When the family member arrives, they let go. So yes. You create your realities, every bit of your realities, from birth to death and everything in between.

Q: That's hard for me. Some things come into our lives that we just know we wouldn't choose. Could you speak to that?

A: When bad things happen to good people, they haven't consciously chosen it. But they have vibrationally chosen it. If you see how the Law of Attraction works, that whatever vibration you put out there is going to be matched by it, you might not say it's something a person consciously chose—for example no one's going to choose to die a painful, awful death from cancer—but they allowed that condition to develop. Many people carry with them throughout their lives, even onto their deathbed, resentments and guilt and worry. That is where all physical illness comes from, from these negative emotions that people nurture even. When you are hoarding all this negativity in your heart, in your gut, in your mind, it's got to have negative effects on your physical body, on your relationships, and on everything in your life.

On the other end of the spectrum, if you're always going around praising people, appreciating them, loving them, looking for the good in them, ignoring all the negative stuff, then you're going to reap the benefits of that also.

Q: Do you think it's good advice for people to be childlike?

A: Absolutely. The wisest you have ever been as human beings is when you were little children. They are just so uninhibited and joyful, and they live in the present moment with joy. They live in the present moment. They're not thinking about what's going to happen ten years from now, or even ten minutes from now. They're living in the present moment with joy, and that is the key. You should all be like little children again; that's the best advice that we could ever give to anybody.

Q: I don't want to get too much into your last life on Earth, but it was said that you died of a broken heart. Is that true?

A: It's been said in the history books, and yes, that was a sad lifetime. It's not something that is a part of us now in the sense that it's important. It's certainly a part of the historical Chief Joseph, but the spirit of that man has grown and evolved far beyond that today. So yes, that was a sad lifetime. Tragic lifetime, in human terms. But it also had its compensations and its joys. Joseph was able to bring the plight of his people to the attention of the governments, so a lot of good came out of it, a lot of new awareness on the part of the whites that perhaps wasn't there before.

Q: When you the historical Joseph died, what was that like when you transitioned over?

A: Transition, or death, is always a pleasant experience.

Q: Always a pleasant experience?

A: We're talking about at the moment you make your transition, not saying that the painful part, if it is painful, is pleasant. Dying is the easiest thing you'll ever do, because you're reemerging back into the world of spirit, back to where you came from, back to your source. It's like a breath of fresh air. It's like taking off a tight shoe. You feel that kind of sense of relief and release, and it's joyful. You'll be inundated with so much joy that if you could get even a small glimpse of what that was like—and you've been there many times, you've all done this many times, but you don't remember it—but if you could get a small glimpse or remembrance of it, you would never fear death again, and you would go through the rest of your lives with a smile on your lips and with joy in your hearts.

> Dying is the easiest thing you'll ever do, because you're reemerging back into the world of spirit . . . back to your source . . . It's like taking off a tight shoe.

Q: I don't actually fear death, in fact I kind of look forward to it. Just maybe not too quickly.

A: Yes, John often says that and we applaud that. We think that's a great perspective to hold.

Q: Why do we keep coming back to Earth to separate ourselves from source, only to reemerge back into source?

A: Because it's a big game. It's fun. Life is supposed to be fun. Whether we're talking about life here in physical form on the planet or whether we're talking about life where we speak to you from. It's supposed to be fun. And so when you, your soul, decided that you were going to come down to Earth again and play around a little bit, it was a conscious, deliberate choice. You did it, not because there's any karma to repay or any past life debts to repay or because you're being punished by being cast into a physical body again. It's simply because you wanted to do it because it would contribute to your overall growth and evolution. So it's a joyful process, that's the intent of your soul.

Q: If we're from source and we're All That Is, really, why do we have to have soul growth?

A: You don't have to have soul growth. Soul growth is simply who you are. You're growing. You're never static. It's not like you're being required by some divine power to grow or that you're commanded to grow. It's just your nature, to grow, to evolve, to change, to have fun in the process of it. The alternative would be to be stale, stagnant, static, and that is not the nature of creation. It's not the nature of being.

Q: I guess pure bliss would still be static, in a sense?

A: We don't see it as static. We said earlier that your higher selves exist in a state of bliss, ecstasy, joy all the time; but they're still growing, and the growth is part of who you are. It's impossible to remain the same. Growing is simply the nature of creation. It's the nature of you, it's the nature of God, it's just your nature to grow and that's a joyful thing as we see it. We realize there are others who will disagree with us, probably many others, but that's our view of it.

Q: I know that all times are special on Earth, but is this time somehow different in some way?

A: It is, but as you said, every moment is special. And every moment is different. This particular time, although it seems your world is going to hell some days, it really isn't. These are not the end times, in our view. This is not the eve of destruction, this is not Armageddon. This is simply a stage in your growth. It's a special time because more and more humans are waking up. And a lot of incentives for that are the so-called disasters that are happening in your world today. People realize that something needs to be changed here. We need to wake up to what's going on. So these are great times, this is the best time in the human race's history to be alive. Many more humans are waking up now than have in the last thousand years.

Q: What does it mean to wake up?

A: To simply remember what it's all about. To remember who you are. To remember who God is, who Goddess is. To remember that life is good. That whether you're dead or alive, life is good. Once everyone, and you will reach this point eventually, maybe not in your lifetimes but it doesn't really matter to you individually, but the human race will reach a point where they have awakened. And once that point is reached, you will be truly able to create heaven on Earth.

Q: What if I want to do it now?

A: You can create heaven on Earth in *your* world, and that's the only place you really have any power anyway. Instead of worrying or being afraid of what's going on in the world around you, just focus on your own world. And bring as much joy and love and appreciation and laughter and fun into your own life as you possibly can. In doing that you will create more joy and love and laughter in the world around you, and even beyond the world to the dimensions of spirit. Each of you, standing alone and fully, consciously aligned with your higher self, is far more powerful than many millions who are living in fear or doubt or anger. One person.

Q: Is there a reason I'm so animated by and drawn to this type of material?

A: Yes. You're very wise.

As you grow as a human being and as a being of spirit, you're becoming more and more aligned with your higher self, with your God self, with your source. When that kind of growth and evolution happens, it's very normal and natural for you to get interested in this kind of airy-fairy stuff. It's perfectly normal. It's good that you're able to run with it and not let the prejudices and negativity of society keep you from doing what you're led to do. Even today with many people waking up there's still quite a bit of prejudice against the sort of thing that we're doing here.

> The antidote to doubt is to know you're in good hands, to know you're safe, to know you're good, to know you're God.

Q: I ignore that.

A: Good. That's the best way to approach it.

Q: We were talking about doubt. Many humans are plagued with doubt. What can they do to transmute that?

A: Doubt is a human thing; it's something that your higher self knows nothing about. The key to overcoming doubt is to trust and have faith that you're in good hands. We'll go beyond faith and trust to say that the antidote to doubt is to know you're in good hands, to know you're safe, to know you're good, to know you're God. We're not saying you can make the leap from a state of deep doubt, in ten minutes or less, to a state of perfect knowing. But we are saying, as we talked about in another context earlier, that you can take it step by step. So let the doubt be okay. Don't beat yourself over the head because you're being doubtful or because you're being human. But know you're in good hands, and know that the doubt will pass, all things pass.

Q: You say we're in good hands. Whose hands are they?

A: Yours. God's.

Q: That's the same thing?

A: Same thing.

Q: Could you speak to that? It's a hard concept to wrap one's mind around.

A: It is. One of the terms that we are fond of for God is "All That Is" because that really says it all right there. God is All That Is. God is not this divine being who sits up there somewhere in the clouds on a throne and dictates to you what your life should be. God does not judge or criticize. God is not a single entity like that. It's the divine energy that permeates everything. We talked earlier about even inanimate objects having that divine energy. And certainly living beings, plants, animals, humans, these are all part of God. God is All That Is and the divine energy of God flows through every part and particle of everything that exists. You as human beings are certainly a conscious part of God. The rocks and the plants don't have that same consciousness, but they do have an awareness of God, an awareness of that divine energy.

We understand it's hard, particularly since so many humans are still part of traditional religion, we realize it's hard for them to accept this concept, and for them to absorb it and assimilate it. That is, in our view, what God is—and so literally you are all God. You're all Goddess. And you have the power that goes along with being divine, even though you don't think you do most of the time.

Q: Does that include instant manifestation?

A: It could. It doesn't usually because of what you talked about a moment ago, David, doubt. But yes, it's possible.

Q: Will there be a point when I can pick up, for instance, a rock or a piece of wood and sort of meld with its energy and have a sort of energetic party with it?

A: Sure. You do that now with other people. And you certainly probably do it if you have a pet. And yes, you can do it with a rock, you can do it with a pet. You can do it with anything. It's particularly easy to do it with a living being like a human or an animal, but yes certainly.

Q: I would like to play a game and have some fun. Could I throw out some words and have you respond to them?

A: Sure.

Q: Joy.

A: It's the purpose of your life. Joy is what it's all about. If you are joyful, you'll thrive. And the more joyful you are, the more abundant you will be. Joy is what it's all about.

Q: Why do we forget that?

A: Because there are so many distractions in your world around you. You don't really forget it; you just lose sight of it. Just like you can never be disconnected from your higher self, you can pinch it off. It's not really forgetting, it's just becoming so distracted and immersed in the worldly stuff that you lose sight temporarily, it's always temporarily, of what it's all about, what you are all about, who you are.

Q: Jesus.

A: A great teacher. No more the son of God, however, than—

Q: —I am?

A: You are. Exactly. A great teacher, yes.

Q: Ascension.

A: That is a word John is uncomfortable with. To us, ascension means . . . everything we've been talking about today is ascension. Growth. Evolution. Remembering who you are. Moving back into that divine energy that you came from. That, to us, is ascension.

Q: 2012.

A: You create your own realities. And so some of you will choose to participate in whatever you think 2012 is about, and some of you will choose not to. The significance we see is that so many people are aware of it now and focusing on it. You do choose, at some level, which of the possible parallel realities you want to experience.

Q: Adolf Hitler.

A: That's a good subject. Everybody who was, what you would call, adversely or tragically affected by the era of Hitler and by Hitler himself was there because they created together, they cocreated that reality that was, from a human perspective, certainly a tragic and sad and awful time in your history. But Hitler was a catalyst for growth in many people who participated in that holocaust. And it really was a holocaust in human terms. So good did come out of that, and Hitler did go to heaven, whatever you conceive heaven to be.

Q: What is heaven?

A: A state of returning to your higher self, to God. It's not a place, it's a state of being, a state of mind if you will. And you can create that heaven here on Earth while you're still in these physical bodies. And you can also—you're very good at this—create hell on Earth when you're still in these physical bodies.

Q: Another concept. Money.

A: Money is energy. Energy is limitless. Money is limitless.

Q: Let's say one had no money and wanted to attract or create a million dollars. How would one go about doing that?

A: Well, most people, especially if they have no money, are not going to be able to attract a million dollars overnight. We talk about doing things in baby steps. To create a million dollars you need to have what we would call an abundance consciousness.

Q: It's hard to get money if you don't have any money?

A: But it's possible. You've probably heard about people who have gone bankrupt and lost everything, after having been quite wealthy, and who are able to restore themselves to a state of wealth fairly quickly. It's because they might have lost their money, but they didn't lose their abundance consciousness. That's where all money comes from. It's simply energy, it's flowing around in the ethers. Once you have an abundance consciousness, you can take that energy and manifest in the form of dollars or any other kind of abundance. Doesn't have to be just money. Certainly someone who's had a poverty consciousness is probably not going to go to an abundance consciousness tomorrow. But it's possible simply by changing yourself one thought at a time. One day at a time. One moment at a time.

One of the best ways, we think, for people who are coming from a poverty consciousness to change that is to look around them and see: what they do have to feel grateful and appreciative for in their life? There is nobody on the planet that is totally destitute of everything. Nobody. There's always some abundance in your life. Maybe you're poor in terms of money, but you have excellent health. Maybe you have great relationships. So look at the things in your life where you are abundant and that will help you to increase your overall consciousness of abundance and that will draw the money in, it must.

Q: There always does seem to be something to be appreciative of. Sometimes I'm taking a bite out of an apple and it's just so juicy.

A: You're surrounded by magnificent abundance, yet so many people don't see that. They're focusing on what's lacking.

Q: Alien abduction.

A: There are no aliens out there, there are only fellow beings. Certainly there is life other than what you know here on planet Earth, but there are no enemies out there, only friends you haven't yet met. For the most part you haven't yet met.

Q: Will they walk among us one day?

A: They are already in a sense. This is a rough comparison, but they're walking among you in the same way that we're walking among you.

Q: You seem like a friend, Chief Joseph. Have I known you before?

A: Yes. We have been together many times. And you are a dear old friend.

Q: If I wanted to speak to you more, or if anyone did, can we contact you?

A: Absolutely. John doesn't have any monopoly on us.

Q: Would it just take intent?

A: Intent, and an openness to receive. It's like opening to any spirit guide. It's really not a lot different, in terms of the energy, from opening up to another human being. You can close yourself off from the people around you, or you can open yourself up. It's the same thing here. If you're open, that person or spirit is going to be responsive.

Q: We've interviewed other beings or entities for this documentary. Do you know them?

A: Yes. We're colleagues. We work together sometimes. Obviously not in this context, but yes, we're all old friends.

Q: Bruce Springsteen.

A: Talented soul. Brings a lot of joy to people.

Q: Who killed JFK?

A: JFK killed JFK. As we said before, everyone chooses the manner and timing of their death. And certainly that was true of him. JFK is fine now.

Q: Free will.

A: The basis of your existence is freedom. You all have free will. So you're free. We realize many people would disagree with us and don't see it like this, but you're all free to do whatever you want. You're free to be whatever you want. You're free to have whatever you want. You're free, free, free. Free will, as we see it, is part of who you are. Even though many of you choose to shackle yourselves and curtail your freedoms, that is a choice too. But you are free.

Q: Is the sum total of our lives sort of the choices we make in each moment of free will?

A: Basically, yes. What you are living today is a result of the choices you made yesterday, ten years ago, twenty years ago. This is a bit of a tangent. We always advocate that people never look back in the way that many people do look back. Like they're saying "if I hadn't made this choice ten years ago then I wouldn't be suffering like I am today." Well, that may be, but because you do have free will you can choose where to go from today. And the choices you make today will create your tomorrow, your next year, the next ten years. So yes, your choices make up everything you have created, everything you are creating, everything you will create. It's all a matter of your choices, what you choose in terms of your thoughts and all the vast array of choices you have available to you.

Q: Is it true that many people live by default and not by conscious choice?

A: Yes, it's true. They're still creators, you're all very powerful creators, but they're creating by simply not choosing what they want. Instead they are focusing on what other people have chosen for them, or they're focusing on the news media, or whatever. You're powerful creators. You create everything you've ever experienced. And the only alternative to that is to make yourself a victim, of fate or whatever, of mother and father's mistreatment, or whatever. Doesn't matter what it is. There are no victims. There are absolutely no victims.

Q: Another concept. Lightworker.

A: We like that. It's a good term because you who are aware and awake spiritually are bringing more light into the world. You are enlightening the world around you and the people around you, and you are setting an example of a happy, joyful life for others. When you are a true lightworker, when you're bringing light into your own life, into the world and people around you, you have a very profound effect.

Q: I feel that this documentary we're making will be filled with light. Reading the energy, do you feel it'll be viewed by a lot of people?

A: Yes. People are ready for this, David. People are ready for this. They're hungry for something. Very often the traditional channels, if you will, are not working. Traditional religion, people are falling away from that. Or if they're remaining in it, they're tailoring it to their own needs and desires. People are hungry for answers. They're hungry for themselves, really— to find out why they're here, who they are, and to know that their lives have purpose and meaning. And so this is going to be a magnificent vehicle for bringing that awareness to so many.

> *You create everything you've ever experienced. And the only alternative to that is to make yourself a victim. . . . There are no victims. There are absolutely no victims.*

Q: I hope so. I hope you don't find this question frivolous, but: Sasquatch?

A: There are no frivolous questions. Delightful being. He kind of comes and goes.

Q: Is it just one being?

A: No, we're not talking about one being. We're talking about the group, if you will. The race. There are many, many life-forms you're not even aware of that exist here, now. Some of them on Earth. Some of them are not necessarily physical, but they're all around you. Sasquatch is just one of those delightful mysteries, if you will.

Q: Can you make it less mysterious?

A: The purpose, as we see it, of these kinds of experiences is simply to give you a broader view of life than you usually have as human beings. To know that there is far more to life even on planet Earth than you can see clearly . . .

Q: How can we connect more with these other life-forms? I feel I'm ready to meet some of them.

A: Then you will. Many people, when they view something like Sasquatch, come at it from a perspective of fear and apprehension. But when you're open to these different life-forms, just like open to a spirit guide, then you can communicate with them and they will be open to you. There's a gap there that cannot be bridged until you do open up to them on a heart level, not from your head.

Q: Now I don't want to make you blush, Chief Joseph. Sex.

A: Oh, we love that subject. Sex is one of the most misunderstood, maligned experiences of the human race. Sex was intended to be one of the most joyful, powerful experiences any human being could ever have. Yet you've shackled it with all these misconceptions and shoulds and should nots, and all these misplaced ideas of what it really is. When you come together in a romantic sexual relationship with another human being, whether it's the same sex or a different sex doesn't really matter in our view, in a spirit of deep caring and love—and again remember how we define love as the choice to see the divinity in all beings—so when you approach a romantic relationship from that perspective, the sex has got to be fantastic. And it should be. But very often people who are open-minded or enlightened, if you will, when it comes to sex feel constrained in their sexual relationships and that kind of mutes the whole experience. Sex is a wonderful, powerful way to communicate with your fellow human beings.

Q: Karma.

A: We do not teach or believe that you have to repay past debts, if you will. And that's what many people see karma being, like your past misdeeds from this life or another lifetime, you gotta make up for those. And that's in our view nonsense. If you want us to be more blunt about it, it's bullshit. We said earlier, all your power is in this present moment. You are not in any way shackled by the past. Past of this life, past of many lifetimes ago. And so there's nothing to repay. All you need to do, in our view, is to know where you want to go from here. It doesn't matter how you may have got here, doesn't matter how many "sins" you may have committed in the past. Karma, we think, causes a lot of people unneeded pain and anguish.

Q: Because of their belief in karma?

A: Because they believe that, for example, their suffering in this lifetime is the result of something they did that they don't even remember. Yeah, it causes pain and suffering. If they have a physical ailment or a deformity and blame it on karma, it's a very unproductive approach to life, because as we said before all your power is right now, so it doesn't matter what happened in the past. All that matters is where you want to go from here, and you have all the power to go wherever you want from here, right here. And now you have that power.

Q: George Bush and Dick Cheney.

A: They've taught you guys a lot. We realize that they are today rather unpopular. We will say that they are doing the best they can. But what they've taught you is a lot about what you don't want, and from that perspective of knowing what you don't want, you can then clarify what you *do* want, and in doing that you are empowered to *create* what you do want. You have to start at home, start with yourself. But George Bush and Dick Cheney are good teachers for all of you.

Q: And they are God also?

A: That's right, exactly. There are no enemies here. If there's an enemy, it's you in your view of yourself. Because you can't see another person as your enemy without coming from some place within yourself where you are your own enemy.

Q: So some place of self-hatred?

A: If you totally accept and love yourself, you will totally love and accept even those that you might otherwise call your enemy. Those you disagree with, those you would like to see, especially public figures, doing something different. It's a matter of seeing the big picture. Imagine how Jesus or God or your higher self would see George Bush and Dick Cheney and that will give you some glimpse of maybe a better way of looking at them.

Q: I have a very important question. Why is the world obsessed with Britney Spears?

A: Celebrities in general evoke a sense of longing in people, a longing for their own greatness. They see these stars as great in whatever way they may be perceived as being great. What is so seductive about them is that people want to see that greatness in themselves. These public figures are serving as catalysts and as teachers to show you that you also are great. You don't have to live your life vicariously through these figures; you can live it joyfully through your own greatness.

Q: Another grand concept. David Thomas.

A: You are truly a delightful old soul, David, and we've known that for a long time. We are delighted that we were able to connect, as it were, sort of in the physical through John. We applaud what you are doing. We think you are a catalyst for the bringing of much more light into the world, and you are attracting already, even though you may not be fully aware of it, people who want what you are creating.

Q: Chief Joseph, I feel as if we should start wrapping up. Is there anything else you'd like to add, maybe some uplifting words for our viewers?

A: The foundation of our work here with John is simply to encourage people to be joyful, to find good in the world around them, to look for it, deliberately look for it. Not just to stumble over it accidentally, but to look for the good first of all in themselves. To be grateful, to be appreciative of the gift of life that they have in these human bodies. All of you are physical extensions of your God selves, and that is a great gift that you were given when you came into physical form. So find the joy in that, find the joy in yourself, find the joy in the people around you. Your loved ones, your friends, your coworkers, look for the good, even in people you may disagree with. George Bush and Dick Cheney. Look for the good in everyone, look for the good in everything. Look for the good. Look for the joy, and you will find joy and good increasing in your own life, and it doesn't get any better than that. That's your purpose, joy. Be joyful. Be joy.

Q: Thank you, Chief Joseph, and I look forward to talking to you again.

A: And thank you, David and Matt. It has been our deep pleasure to be with you today. And now, may the peace of the Great Spirit be with you always and in all ways.

≡

This interview, especially the last third or so, had seemed like a party. Sasquatch? Britney freakin' Spears? This is soil I hadn't really expected to till, but I found myself so comfortable with Chief Joseph that I went free-form.

And it was a bash I didn't want to end. So John joined us in the rental car, and we drove into the country, where Matt shot B-roll footage of the snow-dolloped mountains, vast expanses of pretty land, and languidly loping deer.

> *Look for the joy, and you will find joy and good increasing in your own life, and it doesn't get any better than that. That's your purpose, joy. Be joyful. Be joy.*

We wound up at a steakhouse, then hit The Irma, a downtown hotel built by Wild Bill Hickok back in the day. It still had that old-timey feel, and while Matt and John enjoyed a brew, I was pleased to discover a poker game at a table in the back room of the bar, which was called the Silver Dollar Saloon.

Texas hold 'em was being dealt by a gargantuan

creature with a linebacker's broad shoulders and a serious demeanor. He had to be six-foot-four and weigh at least three hundred pounds. The person was dressed in Old West garb and looked like someone not to be messed with. It was only on second glance—well, maybe even third—that I discovered that this was actually a woman. Not to be mean, but she was truly about the size of a bison, and all muscle. I had never seen a person like this in my entire life, and her gruff manner made me even more apprehensive.

But there was a seat open and I love poker, so I sat. And played. John came over and said his farewells. I played longer. Matt went back to the motel.

I drank beer and played poker with the locals for hours. When I told them that I was in town to interview Chief Joseph for a documentary, most looked at me askance. No one said anything overtly denigrating, which I found refreshing, but I could tell they all thought that the guy from Los *Angeles* talking to dead people was a weirdo.

I simply took this in genial stride, allowed them their opinions, and focused on the good, just as Chief Joseph had counseled. The beer was cold and slaking. Poker is fun. I was winning. This hulking dealer, who went only by the name "Calamity Jane," was of an ilk I'd never encountered before, and likely never would again. I studied her as Margaret Mead might have viewed a new tribe she was studying. So it was, in fact, all good.

The bar closed and the game broke up. I asked if anyone knew the number of a taxi company. Then something happened that surprised me. Calamity Jane told me she'd give me a ride out to the Motel 6.

I quickly analyzed the situation. Was she going to rob

me of the $215 I'd just won? Would she demand sexual favors, perhaps the crushing kind, in exchange for the ride? Would she extract a buck knife from her deerskin boots and use it for some unspeakable backwoods ritual?

Of course not. She was a human offering help to another human. Natural as could be. So I drove with Calamity Jane in her red pickup truck back to the motel, not talking much—she wasn't the loquacious type—but simply sharing the brisk, cloudless Cody night with a new friend.

Six

Lee Carroll Channeling Kryon

The following week, back in L.A., we were scheduled to interview the sixth and final channeler. Matt was now so excited about the project that he was even enthusing to his film business associates about the movie. "I can tell they think it's a bit odd," he said. "So I just say, 'wait and see it! This stuff is awesome!'" I had to smile; he was now just about as thrilled about channeling as I. A convert . . . Matt was a convert.

Lee Carroll was perhaps the most renowned channeler in the project, with book sales of more than a million copies and countless followers worldwide. I'd listened to hours of recordings of him channeling a being named Kryon. I'd read reams of text. So I already knew that the Kryon style was somewhat more professorial than I was used to.

During lectures, for example, Kryon never takes questions from the audience, and up until now he'd rejected being interviewed on camera by anyone, anytime, anywhere. So I was actually surprised—and beyond delighted—when Lee and Kryon agreed to participate in the project. I would find out during the interview exactly why they'd agreed to the taping.

Lee took the train from his home in Escondido, near San Diego, to L.A., and Matt picked him up and drove him in the light February rain to his little apartment just off Hollywood Boulevard. A friend had agreed to let us use her Beverly Hills house to shoot the interview, but at the last moment she'd cancelled, so I was hoping Lee wouldn't mind the unadorned venue.

Striding back and forth in Matt's sparse living room, hands clasped behind his back and wearing a baby blue cable knit sweater, Lee seemed the unlikeliest of channelers. If a sixty-four-year-old can be described as "preppy," that was what Lee was, though he certainly wasn't the condescending brand of preppy. He was curious and peppered Matt and me with questions about our own lives.

I was again struck by how youthful this channeler looked, and asked him about that. "Well," he said, "Kryon has told me that when I am in trance state, when I am actually channeling, the aging stops. I don't age at all. And I've been doing this since 1989, not channeling every day of course, but quite a lot. So I'm sure it has slowed the aging process for me."

Matt turned on the lighting, readied the cameras, and Lee took his seat on the couch, me opposite him in a chair. Lee was relaxed as a kitten, but I was slightly nervous, perhaps wanting to impress Kryon when he came through since I knew I was the first to ever interview him. But first I wanted to find out about Lee's life as a channel.

"See, twenty years ago I thought that all of these esoteric things were for older women over forty and that they would have nothing to do with men," Lee explained. "So I was dragged to these two guys who channeled for me, and there was *something*—this was three years apart. They both told me the same thing. That is when I had to start looking at how two guys twenty years apart in age, three years apart in when they told me, who never knew each other, could get me information that was identical. And the information just happened to be that there was a master named Kryon who I was supposed to get ahold of."

Was he at all apprehensive or dubious?

"Of course I felt all of that," he said. "I was an audio engineer for many years. I didn't like people much. I preferred to spend most of my time in a sound booth, and I liked it that way. I wasn't particularly well-read, wasn't an orator, and I certainly had very little, if any, interest in metaphysics or spiritual matters."

And yet here he was two decades later, speaking to packed houses around the world and even having Kryon talk at the United Nations several times.

"I followed what can only be described as the urgings of my soul. It was just something I *knew* I was supposed to be doing. I didn't know then why, but it felt right. I now know this is a pre-birth agreement I made to be the human vessel for Kryon here on Earth. Though I'm not the only one; others also channel him publicly, though I believe I'm the only one in this country."

Even after having been a channeler for several years, Lee still had certain misgivings . . . not about the channeling itself, but about letting people in his personal life know what he was up to.

"Well, I have several families, as many of us do, and

I have more than one marriage," he explained. "The wife that I have now I was introduced to in the recording studios. And I was on my third Kryon book at the time. And so we dated for a long time before I ever opened my mouth about what I was doing. And I remember the day—we were going to go have spaghetti. And we never made it to the spaghetti place because I brought my books. I said, 'It's now or never. She's got to know.' Because I felt—I felt my heart and what was going on. And I said, 'I've got to—it's either make it or break it right now.' So I brought my books to her house, and we never got out of there. Because she actually said, she took it all in, and she said, 'I'm going to have to think about it.' She read the books and called me up and said, 'This is everything I've always believed.'"

With that, we were ready for the special presence of Kryon, so Lee closed his eyes, took one long, deep breath, and exhaled. A few seconds later, a louder, deeper voice was speaking, and Lee's face, indeed entire body, was more animated.

"Greetings, dear one, I am Kryon," said the voice.

Even this early in the encounter, as I asked if he had any opening statement, I could feel a confident and powerful, yet somehow not overwhelming, energy emanating from the being. If Tobias had seemed like a brother, Kryon was more strong-but-kindly uncle.

≡

A: There is no such thing as an opening statement for Kryon, but there is a statement in real time, in now time. Says that what is taking place right here, the thing that you are capturing with your technology, is that step that we told you could very well happen in this new energy. It is one of many steps that you can experience and expect where the human being is guided to a place where he will serve other human beings with integrity. Where they can see for themselves what is and what is not up regarding this which you call channeling, which we call the love of God, which communicates with humans through humans. So indeed this is the opening statement, and I would say blessed is the human being who is watching this at the moment who has an open mind and has the integrity and spirit to ask, "Is God bigger than I thought? Will I continue to watch? Could this be real?"

Q: Could you explain a little bit about who you are?

A: Kryon is the name that I have chosen to give for numerological reasons to the entity which is an angel and is your brother and your sister and whom you know when you're not on the planet. When you're not here on Earth, I know you and I know your name. You are a piece of the whole, which you call God. So think of me as a brother, as a sister, as an angelic presence—not as an authority, never to be worshiped. I am one who steps into your dimension through my partner, who is Lee. I am one who gives information to make your life better with suggestions that will bring you closer to what you call God, with suggestions that would bring you more into the universal system of what you have called cocreation. Therefore you would say I am Kryon, lover of humanity.

Q: You often refer to yourself as Kryon "of magnetic service." What does that mean?

A: I am the first to give you the messages regarding the magnetic grid of the planet being that which communicates in an interdimensional way with your DNA. What you do not know and your science has not yet discovered is that DNA is also magnetic. The actual double helix and the attributes of the chromosomes within it are in a loop. And this loop has electric current running through it just as much of your synapse does in your bodies. Therefore anything that has current and a loop running through it creates a magnetic field. It is small but it is dynamic. The field is created through superconductivity, that is to say that there is much that goes through the loop even without the power source that you might expect. This magnetic field you have as a human being intersects the magnetic field which is that of the Earth, both of them very small. This creates what you have called an electronics induction. Induction therefore is the description of communication between two overlapping magnetic fields.

The magnetic field of your planet was altered from 1989 to the year 2002, recorded by your scientists. It moved more in those ten years than it had in the past hundred. This is what we said would take place when I came in; it's about lifting the veil. It's about a new way of communicating with your DNA. It's regarding the preparation to year 2012. Therefore, because this is my specialty, I have been called that of magnetic service. It is truly a name which is not understood, started out to be perhaps part of a metaphor, but stuck nevertheless.

Q: Do you know who is going to be viewing this movie?

A: Dear one, I know who is looking right now. And to you it has not yet even been completed. The potential for the eyes that are on this screen at the moment are known to me. All the potentials in the now are known. Those watching right now I will say, "I know your names, I know the potential that you might indeed put this media in and see it, to be at the synchronistic right time to see it. And I have to say to you, knowing all the things that might have brought you here: What are you going to do with it?" Very, very difficult to explain to any creature in the third dimension, on Earth, how there is no fortune-telling, but the potentials are all there. So if you are one now watching it, and you are, there was the potential all along you would, and I know who you are because of it.

Q: Kryon, if we're all masters, why do we decide to come to Earth and hide our mastery?

A: You have just asked the question, "what is life about?" This is covered over and over. So many communications, so many channelings through the years trying to explain to the human being why angels, as you are, would come to the Earth disguised as human beings on this even playing field, forgetting who they are. Working through a scenario that is so difficult sometimes, so challenging sometimes, so rewarding sometimes. It is because there is a test on this planet. This is the only planet of free choice, and there are billions of planets. The only one in the universe at the moment to have pieces of God disguised as human beings living upon its surface. It is a system. What happens at the end of a certain amount of time will be measured. For Gaia, being that of the energy of the Earth is related to you, and what you do with your vibration will also affect Gaia. And at the end of the test a measurement will be taken. Angels cannot make this decision on their own. God cannot make this decision because God is biased in love. Therefore it is a test unbiased of vibrational increase or decrease. At the end of this time, in the very distant future when humans choose not to be humans anymore, the vibration will be then applied to a new creation, a new universe which will have your stamp upon it.

I have just given you an overview, which doesn't help your life at all. It is simply one for curious human beings who want to know what is it about, who want to know why there are challenges, and indeed the very question why, as a piece of God, why you would come and do this.

It is why the Kryon washes your feet. It is why I love those who are here. For you are the ones who decided to do the difficult work. And I would like to tell you, most of you who would watch this without bias, right now, have been here before, and know what this is about internally. And you are the ones who will return yet again to do some more.

Q: If we've been here before and are such masters, why is there such frustration at certain points?

A: Frustration is built in with what you would call the duality. You cannot have a test without a puzzle. The puzzle is the duality. The duality is represented as a multidimensional multifrequency of dark and light. And when you come in, you're presented with this puzzle. You with free choice can go any direction you choose, and many go in directions that actually create the drama—which creates the challenge. It is up to them to either get out of it or stay in it, and there you have the free choice of the human being, there you have the learning.

> This is the only planet of free choice, and there are billions of planets.

Therefore the answer to your question is: You come in already to a difficult playing field where the energy is not commensurate with your divinity. And that, my friend, has caused the wars, the frustrations, the lack of integrity, the dishonesty, and many of the things you wallow in that you wish were better. And that, my friend, oh dear one, that is the potential of this planet. Listen to me. The potential of this planet is grander than anything you've ever seen. It includes peace on Earth. It includes those who will solve problems in that which you call the Middle East. The unsolvable will become solvable.

This is why the Kryon is here, to tell you that the energy

that you sit in now is increasing. Those who will follow in your path, those indeed who are being born every day and who work here, you might say, of this planet Earth, as a child are seeing a new energy, and they have a new consciousness. Watch for it, that is the answer.

Q: So children in a sense sort of have it figured out. Is there hope for us who are a little older?

A: You are seeing evolution take place. You are seeing it grandly, the actual shift in DNA. You're actually seeing children who will have a different attitude than any children have had before. That is understandable in an evolving species. You are asking whether you as an older human being can change, and the answer is absolutely and yes, for you can become childlike. You can become as they are. All you have to do is have the intent to shift the energy. That has always been the lesson. They're coming born with it; you must learn it. This is the teaching of Kryon, always has been, how a human being in any situation, in any energy, with any challenge or any problem can take and rework their lives to find the piece of God that is inside and have then the light they deserve.

Q: Was I born with that innocence and now I have to be reminded of it?

A: Humans think they are born clean. They would love to think they are unbiased. It is not the case. Think for a minute of your animals. You will freely admit in an animal species that they come in with instinct. They can lose their parents at a very early age and yet they will know who their enemies are, what to eat, what the poisons are, where to go, where to fly in order not to be cold. They come in with instinct, and so does the human. The human comes in with the instinct that some have called karma—not entirely accurate—with a blueprint and a set of what they've experienced before that some will have to either continue with or unlearn. So you do not come in on an equal playing field. You come in with a predisposed set of challenges to work through. It's part of the duality.

Q: Why would we choose to do that over and over again?

A: The process is this: When the human being goes beyond a challenge that is given to him, a new energy is produced that helps the planet. Now you probably understand a little more. So as you undo the things that [you] were predisposed to see and wallow in, and conquer them, the benefactor is not only you but those around you and also Gaia itself. So there's an engine of change, you might say, which is human beings who then void their drama. Human beings who walk through the challenge. And this energy can even be felt. I challenge you to go through something like this and not feel it. On the other side of this challenge which you have voided is euphoria. It is an epiphany, a hug from spirit, and you know you've done something spectacular. So therefore the answer to your question is this: You come in predisposed to work the challenges, and as you work them and solve them and conquer them, Gaia is the beneficiary.

Q: You say the Earth is the only planet of free choice among billions.

A: That is the truth.

Q: Why is that or how does that work?

A: There is a grand scheme. A scheme that is far beyond what anything you think would be. This grand scheme is known by you. So thin is the veil that separates full knowledge from yours. You willingly come in to work the grand scheme. I've explained enough of it to you so you will know that what happens here actually will change something else in what you call your future. It has to do with a universal scale, another universe. There are universes being created all the time. Universes are created through shifts of dimensions.

There is no such thing as the Big Bang, and someday your scientists will see that. The residue that you measure in space that you think was the Big Bang was a P-shift; everything happened at the same time. That is an attribute of an interdimensionality. It is not an attribute of the timeline that you call the Big Bang. Universes are born all the time, and each one must have a starting energy. This is part of a plan that has been with us for eons. In this universe from the very beginning it was known that there would be an Earth. That angels would inhabit it. That it would be the only place like that. That there would be more intelligence around the universe, and there is, but this is the only place that has what is going on that you have called "the test." Although you may not understand the reasons why, we say to you there is integrity in it, there is love in it, there's grandness in it, and on the other side of the veil you know all about it.

Q: So it is true that every human on Earth is an angel . . .

A: Every human on Earth is an angel.

Q: Why don't we understand that and live that?

A: The duality is what is being defined as that which keeps you from knowing your angeldom. And it is seemingly an oxymoron, for you say we have a test to perform; why shouldn't we know more about who we are? We have said this before. If it was intuitive, what you had going on on this planet, we might as well just turn on the lights and everyone goes home. You see, there must be secrets, there must be an overlay, there must be a veil, there must be the predetermined energy that says "can't be so." This creates a little mountain to climb, does it not? Those who watch this video, those who have this broadcast into their homes, those who are watching this now, be aware that this is part of the mountain to climb. For it has to do with your belief. What you've been told as opposed to what you feel.

I'll tell you this so that you know a simple answer to all of these things. The love of God is at work. It's personal. It's about you. It's grand. There is healing that is possible even within your own life. Relationships that can be solved. All of these things which you make so challenging and you have all these rules about are all wrapped up in a bigger universe, and yet it comes down to the love within a single human heart. Yes, you're all angels.

> *You see, there must be secrets . . . there must be a veil, there must be the predetermined energy that says, "can't be so." This creates a little mountain to climb, does it not?*

Q: Could the entire process be more graceful and easy, or do we want these challenges?

A: It comes in with an energy where free choice is the king. You might have said "could it be easier?" Absolutely. Free choice, however, took it to a lower energy, where greed and lack of integrity, dishonesty, and the desire for power were the king. It always was. And if you look at Earth and the development of Earth, you will see that this became, for so many centuries, the way of it. Could it have been easier? Oh yes, with a different free choice. Even those on the other side of the veil who are God—and you would say we would see the whole picture, you would say, "well, you would have known"—and we say this: nothing is known about the free choice of the humans on this planet.

We know about the potentials, but not one angel or entity, not even Kryon, can tell you what might happen tomorrow. It is about what the angels do on this planet with their free choice that shapes everything. Could it have been easier? Yes. Could you have done a better job? Define "better job."

Q: Now, what kind of heart energy should one project, not only to help others but to have a better life oneself?

A: You sit in the energy of a Great Shift. Many of you are feeling it; maybe that's why you're watching this now. Maybe there's something that has happened in your life that would allow you for a moment just to open your mind and look inside something you always thought was untenable before, only reserved for those on the lunatic fringe before. And here you find instead wisdom pouring out. Perhaps you'll even feel the love of God pouring out. What we want to tell you is this: There's so much here that is hiding, but you must feel it.

There has been such a shift in these past years, especially in the last twenty or so. Since the year 1987 and what we have called the Harmonic Convergence, all manner of things have shifted. There've been integrity issues that have been solved. There've been large countries whose governments have fallen over when no one expected it. There has been peace between former enemies, and there will be more. There are things here that will grasp you and try to pull you backwards, there is the challenge of what you would call the media, which always wishes to pull you in to the worst thing that is happening on the planet instead of the best. It's up to you to know this, that there is far more going on than you know that is positive, that is loving.

You are in an energy shift and some of you can feel it. For there is so much shift on its way to giving you what the Mayans had predicted, that is a signpost coming in the year

2012 which will move into a new vibration for the planet Gaia. Not a flashbulb experience, but a slow growth into an age which they have called the "age of the yellow sun." In the Mayan writings you will see they are ones who measure the vibration of the planet—not solstices, not equinox. They were about an esoteric level of enlightenment for the Earth, and 2012 is the beginning of the upshift, and you are right on schedule. Watch this, dear ones, look for good things. The answer is: Things are changing.

Q: Can a person deliberately and consciously raise their vibration, and how?

A: Any individual who so wishes to can consciously raise their vibration. And it is so simple. Human beings want to compartmentalize everything. They want to know the steps of ascension. They want to know, itemization by itemization, what things they must do in order to please God. Never understanding that if they are pieces of God themselves there is a switch inside that is all ready to go. That switch is pure intent. Not passive intent, not curiosity, but pure intent. It is the human saying: "Dear God, show me what it is I need to know, I'm ready." And he means it. The switch is thrown. That switch, known very well in spirituality all over the planet, is the one that gives you permission for the epiphany. For the enlightenment to begin, to pour in. For answers. It is slow and you must unlearn what you have been taught, but it is true. Any human can, no matter what the situation, no matter where they are or who they are, through pure intent. So the answer is to begin the process with pure intent, then stand back and watch the shifts and synchronicities as they occur. And then go with them.

Q: For me personally I feel that switch has been thrown. But

I feel regression and frustration as well. How does one deal with that?

A: Do not misinterpret regression and frustration as failure. For sometimes regression is vacation. But those on a mission never think of that. They think perhaps when they are allowed to vacation and not plow forward with the things they think are going to happen, they have failed. Take for instance what you have considered the frustrations at some of the failures, which in your case happen to be when things did not happen when you thought they would. And in this particular case we say the synchronicity was not ready. Therefore, you are on vacation. Honor the synchronicity. Your time is not God's time.

I have another message for you. Reality yells, but faith whispers. That's the

> *What you do here changes the planet. What is happening in this small room changes the planet.*

duality for you. And when you center yourself, the reality you have will whisper, and so you'll have two whispering things that are equal, and so you'll have a lot better time understanding what's failure and what's just waiting.

Q: In terms of this documentary I had a whisper and then a yell, so I feel it's synchronistic . . .

A: It is synchronistic. Everything that's happening in the room is synchronistic. It has to happen sometime, it must begin somewhere. This will not be what you call the end-all of what you're doing. And indeed it will lead you to bigger things. And they may not all be like this. That is the synchronicity, it is the integrity of your path. For you will be able to look back and say, "I was the first one to do this, in this fashion." It will be meaningful. What you do here changes the planet. What is happening in this small room changes the planet. Because a few people doing good things with the synchronicity and integrity of their heart changes so much.

Q: Wow, I got a chill. Is there an entourage that has gathered here?

A: Yes, the Kryon has an entourage that is uncountable. It is because the entourage is not compartmentalized. If soup suddenly showed up in the room, you could not say how many soups are there. That is the way it is with interdimensional things. It is like the soup. And if you flavor the soup, you flavor all the soup—not one piece of it. So what we say is that the entourage of Kryon is like that. It is an energy field but it is made up of entities, and you call it the entourage of Kryon. And it comes in not because Kryon is here; it comes in because *you're* here.

Q: I love some of your word choices that I've heard in other channelings. What is "the wind of birth"?

A: The wind of birth is Kryon's description, the best I can do, to describe that amazing experience on the other side of the veil when a human is going to be born. This is actually the time at which the birth canal opens and the human enters and breathes. This is a point in time in which I see you, and I did in your case as well. Both of you. When you stood there ready to come back into the planet again. And to me it seems that there's a howling wind coming through a huge opening where literally hundreds and thousands of you are making this choice every moment. It's like you lean into this wind which you call 3D, and there's never a moment's hesitation. You're ready to go and hide the magnificence that you are, pretend to be a human for yet another lifetime. I look into your eyes and I say yet again, "Are you ready?" And you say, "I wouldn't miss it." And in you go. It's the wind of birth. To me, something I will never do, something I never have done. But I see the heroes called angels do it. I'm there now.

Q: Why would you never do it yourself?

A: I am not that kind of an angel. There are energies of angels that you would call specialists. We're not compartmentalized to that degree for we're all one, but we take our tasks and we do certain kinds of things for one another. And in that you might say some then come into the planet and some then are support. There are far more supporters than there are humans who come in. I am a supporter.

Q: I've heard it said that only the best and brightest are on Earth now. Is that true?

A: In a sense, yes. But also the worst villains you've ever had are back for another chance. And some of them might surprise you. No, you are all the same. You keep coming around, you go, but here is an attribute I will tell you about. You should know this, for this is very 3D, and you should understand this. Each time you make a vibrational shift for the Earth, let us say each time you conquer a fear, let us say each time you discover something about timing, your spiritual jar fills up a little inside. This spiritual jar is your Akash, it keeps track of the energies that you solve. And when you come back in the next time, all of that is ready at the same level you left it; you never have to relearn it. Many will never open the closet that would expose that which is their esoteric self. We have shamans walking around, we have the past Buddhas walking around, who will never be Buddhas and never be shamans. But it's there. All their life experience is there.

Free choice determines whether they will open the closet, and when they do, you will find them putting upon everything they have learned. This is how you can have someone who is completely untrained in spiritual things suddenly become a master. It seems to be out of the way things work—they have paid their dues, and they have studied, and they've had lifetimes of learning just like you've had.

Q: If we're parts of God, why do we have to learn anything?

A: It is about the Earth, it is about what is going to be in the universe to come, as I have said—so you're really not learning anything as an angel. You are participating in the experience of learning in order to help the planet and beyond. So the learning is the engine, you would say, of the vibrational shift of the planet. It is the way it will always be.

Q: Another phrase I like is "sing your name in light." What does that mean?

A: It is a metaphor for what it is like on my side of the veil. For on yours, everything is limited, severely limited. The difference in limitations between you, for instance, in a human and what you would see as bacteria in a dish. That is how different it is. On my side of the veil your name is not spoken, it is sung. It is sung in all the frequencies together, in light, in harmonies that you cannot imagine, in sonorities that do not exist on the planet, in chord structures that you could only dream about. And each name sounds that way; they sing them together, which may seem complicated to you, but they all harmonize. And so when I say to you that I will sing your name in light someday, it is my way of saying you are grand, you are magnificent, you are a piece of God.

Q: It makes me want to go there now.

A: Indeed there is a cap put upon the human psyche, that a balanced human will never take their own life. And you know that is so in all religions, it has even been called something evil, inappropriate. And that is on purpose as well, you come in with that knowledge that it is inappropriate, perhaps even sacredly inappropriate, and no one will do it for the sake of going to the other side unless there is imbalance or unless one human being has talked them into it.

Q: But I've also heard it said that all deaths are suicides because people choose their time of death. Don't they on some level?

A: At some level death is chosen. This is very interesting that you would bring this up, for when you come to the planet there is a predisposition, you might say a groove that you would travel in, that has upon it a potential of your time of death. It is the human being who understands, however, that they can pop out of that groove and go in another direction with their own free will, which means that they will never meet their death in the groove. Therefore we are saying this, that although death is a potential around you all the time and on some level that potential is known, you are still in control on this planet of your life in a grand, grand fashion. There is no predetermined time that you are going to die. You will choose it at the moment by free choice, in real time, in 3D.

Q: So all deaths are suicides because you choose them . . .

A: If you define suicide as chosen death, I would say yes. Suicide, however, has a very unpleasant connotation. Why don't you say instead it is a chosen journey to home?

Q: You've said the ascended masters are back; are they here physically?

A: In fact they are here now. Those who have expected the

second coming of the Jesus creature, which is the messiah of some, who's the brother of others, and who is a Jew, are here. He is here. And when they expected his second coming in this energy, they were right. Those who expected the ascended masters Elijah and one of the first Buddhas to be here at this time, are right. Even those who saw the ascension on the temple mount of Mohammed and expect his return are right. All of these have occurred. They are all on what you would call the crystalline grid of the planet. This is interdimensional, you're not going to find it, don't dig for it. You will not see the historical Jesus walking down your street one day or holding a press conference.

It is something that says there is an ascended energy on this planet which is here. And so all of these things that have been given to these various religions are indeed so. They've happened, but not in the terminology or in the third dimensionality, that they would have wished. And this is indeed part of why this planet is in grand shift, for this master energy, if you wish, is available, not competitive, for everyone to touch. And it's called the love of God.

Q: Is it actually inside of us?

A: If you wish it to be. That is free choice.

Q: If one wanted to be more connected to what we call God, what are some of the methodologies and ways that one could do that?

A: When you start the journey of connection, there are physical things that you might do at first. You might decide that the best thing to help you tune is to meditate. And you'd be right. For you would tune out those things in your brain where the tapes play, as they say. Where the reality plays, as they say. And so deep meditation might be the part that you would start with to start the pipeline going. And so this is what we would recommend to those just starting—that is to take this time to be quiet. But in the process of your learning there will be the temptation for you to start asking all manner of questions. "What should I do next? Why am I here? Why is this happening? What do I do here, what do I do there?"

And this might sound like a reasonable thing to ask of anyone, especially of spirit on the other side of the veil, and yet I will tell you again: there's only one question you should ask. It's the fast track, as they say, to spirituality. It is the fast track, as they say, to getting whatever it is that you have come for. It is one question and that is: "Dear God, tell me what it is I need to know?"

And this question will open the door for synchronicity you may never have thought of in your laundry list of questions you have for God. So therefore we say to this human being who would be watching this now: whatever is before you and whatever challenges are there, the fast track through all that is to get into a meditative state with pure intent, and say to God, to spirit, "I love you, I know you're there, show me what it is I need to know." And don't expect an answer to fall upon you in a physical way, but instead expect that you have connected to what seems to be the chaos of the system of the universe. Connected in such a way that the synchronicity will begin to appear in your lives like little open doors here and there to guide you to the places that will answer the questions that you would have had otherwise.

Q: Do you then somehow have to keep the connection going, or is it made then?

A: You've just asked the big question. As the energy moves forward, are things going to change? Do you really need to open and close the connection? Is it truly like what you would do in communications on a telephone, opening and closing the connection? Say hello and goodbye? And the answer is "no." For this energy is promoting an ongoing 100 percent constant connection. It is something that all humanity can have. It will not mean that you will move from place to place in challenge. Hardly. It means that you will move from place to place in peace. That is to say you will be at peace with yourself; you will have answers come when they need. You will seem to be an ordinary person, but an ordinary person without drama. One who has answers when they need it, and one who meditates perhaps fewer times because the door is always open. You will not appear to be odd or strange but you will know the door is open. And that is being promoted by the new energy and shift upon you.

> *The fast track through all that is to get into a meditative state with pure intent, and say to God, to spirit, "I love you, I know you're there, show me what it is I need to know."*

Q: Is there such thing as walking meditation?

A: Absolutely, all the time, even while driving. Be careful, but it is indeed there. Many have said it's the angels who take care of you as you're doing these things. The actual answer is it is a state which you are not aware of. You are aware of a state of meditation, a state of sleep, a state of awareness, a state of awaking, perhaps even visions. It's beyond any of those. It's where all of your body knows everything that's going on around it, completely and totally, even in conversation. But there is a third language which is upon you, another pipe that you might imagine is right in the pineal, that is the third eye, the ascension pipe that is always there giving you the answers and the questions and all the things you need to exist at the same time you are in 3D.

Q: Kryon, you seem like a real friend, more than most humans actually. Are we familiar?

A: Very. Let me tell you something, dear one. My partner sits in the chair because you called him. And he would have said "no" to any other human being but you. You were targeted to be here. By your own free will you followed that path, you made the connection at the right time, and I interceded for you. Do not make any judgments about this project beyond finishing it.

Q: Like as far as how many people might see it, or . . .

A: Do not make any judgments around anything. Finish it and let the synchronicity take its course and do not in your own way decide what the timing will be.

Q: That has been a problem; I try to force certain things.

A: Indeed.

Q: Well, in that regard what would you recommend especially for me?

A: Watch the doors open and close like this one has. If the timing bogs down for you, put it away until it is time. But always move forward with it, talk to the right people about it. And let it grow at its own pace in the way it should. You may have some surprises, like the one that sits in front of you right now. You see, things are not always as they seem. There's a bigger plan and you don't know what it is, but you fit into it in such a perfect way when you let go and let it be.

Q: So a big word might be "trust"?

A: Indeed many have said "faith." And we say this again. Not just for you. Faith and trust are so alive that the 3D life you live shouts at you and faith and trust whisper. When you can take your 3D life and balance it with the trust and the faith, that is when things start to happen. You're going to have to suppress what you think is your perception of the way things work. You're going to have to suppress what you've been told about God. You're going to have to put these things at a level where you can finally hear this beautiful voice whispering, that has always been there within you, that says, "I am God, I've got answers, open a pipeline." It is there for you.

Q: Seems resonant to me that one should be heart-based and live from their heart, but what does that really mean?

A: What it means to each human being is different. What we say is that there must be a balance between the intellect and what you would call the heart. And that person who is balanced, that human who is balanced will show. You will know them for they will seem to be more gentle. They would seem to be more open and less judgmental. This is the balance. You might say, "well, they are heart-based." They are not; they are balanced. Never throw away what your truth is, never throw away what your logic tells you, but temper it with the emotion of your heart and become balanced. And then these things will come together.

> The day you start suppressing what you've been told and opening the door to what God really is, in will come God, and it'll have your face on it.

Q: I guess it's hard to put into 3D words, but how do you describe or define God?

A: Difficult. But my immediate answer is "you." My immediate answer is my brothers and my sisters who I've watched come here for eons. The viewers don't like that, the watchers don't like that, because they wish to put God on a pedestal and they want to say all good things come from God and they are taught they are nothing from birth. And it's not that way. Magnificent, all of you. My definition of God are the ones I sit in front of. You want God to be one thing, for you are in 3D. You want to worship God, for you are in 3D. I tell you this: The day you start suppressing what you've been told and opening the door to what God really is, in will come God, and it'll have your face on it.

Q: That is stunningly beautiful. So I suppose it would be true that there is no higher power in the universe than ourselves.

A: And that, my dear friend, is what humans will never accept, but you have said so and it is so.

Q: We'll never accept it? Then why are we here?

A: You will never accept it because it is too grand. It doesn't fall within the purview of duality. Therefore it will never be accepted as a global phenomenon, that you are the highest power that exists. Most of humanity will always select something they believe is higher. Less than one half of one percent of this planet will believe that they are God. That is the difficulty of the duality until the planet itself becomes ascended. Expect this, do not judge it, it is not a negative thing. It's not even a challenge. It's just the way things are. Do not look at this in a negative fashion.

Q: What if I know that I'm a master but I don't seem to be exhibiting it on an earthly plane?

A: Two kinds of humans know they are masters. Ones that know they are masters and are going toward the goal of discovering it any way they can, perhaps making steps and missteps. The other kind of human knows that they are masters absolutely, and by free choice choose not to be. Basically those are the two. There is free choice, but those who absolutely know that they are masters cannot un-know it; therefore I will say, "blessed is the human who knows who they are and moves forward." The ones who choose to move backwards may do so in free choice, but they will indeed be unbalanced and in denial. These are the ones who will spin in drama, find things that are dramatic to occupy their lives so they do not have to think about the shamans that they are. Maybe a longer, convoluted answer than you wanted, but it is so.

Q: Kryon, are you optimistic about the fate of the Earth and humans?

A: What I see, what I teach, and what I know are the potentials of humanity on this planet. The potentials that are most likely to occur based on the energy of right now glow. Look at it this way. When you go to the other side of the veil and you look at the giant billion, trillion parts of humanity all making decisions, the ones that glow the most are the ones that have the highest potential of taking place. And in that is the soup of what you would call predictions.

I do not make predictions—I tell you about potentials, and when I go out there the potentials at this moment are of a planet that is in the process of healing itself very slowly over a long period of time, but taking it to a place that no one ever expected, where there will be no more war. Yes, I am encouraged. That's the reason I am here, I am saying to you, all of you, anyone listening, there is hope here, more than you think. That is the potential of the planet.

Q: Could I throw out a few words for you to comment on? For instance, lightworker?

A: Lightworker is the human being who chooses to take on a high vibration and send light to the planet.

Q: Joy.

A: Joy is an intuitive inner child feeling that is for every single human being a reward for their work. It is in their DNA, it is the essence of God, and so many humans suppress it.

Q: Love.

A: Love is everything.

Q: Hate.

A: Hate is everything.

Q: Could you speak more to that concept?

A: Love and hate are two polarities of duality that exist in an equal amount when you are born; you can choose any one of them you wish. The love quotient is active, the hate quotient is passive. That is to say you could have a room that is dark, but when you put light in it, the whole room is then no longer dark. But if you had a light room and a piece of darkness walked in, nothing would happen. So what I am saying is that both are everything to humanity. It is what you do with it that makes the difference. Now, universally, love is the essence, literally, of atomic structure. Hate is something that humanity creates from their own being. So when I speak of love and hate being everything, my context is in the duality that you face.

Q: Are some extraterrestrials trying to help us?

A: There are many who have already helped, and you will find those in what you would call the Seven Sisters, which are the Pleiadians, for they are the ones who helped alter your DNA originally. This is a very long story and one that needs to be told carefully and with those who have ears that are more receptive than the ones who are listening now.

Q: Sex.

A: One of the most profound and proper and beautiful attributes of human beings. Two enlightened human beings who definitely have the pipeline open to spirit, when engaged in this practice actually can change the vibration of the planet itself. It was created to express love. It happens to be the procreation method. But the act with the heart is one that has been literally unexplored to this day. It is divine.

Q: What might be the optimal human diet?

A: The optimal human diet is the one that the human being will choose on his own. Make no mistake, there is no such thing as a generic human being. You come from such a different platform, different lives, different cultures, and you arrive in this culture. Some of you may wish to only eat one kind of thing, some of you may wish to eat another. Do what your body feels best, with that results in the most energy and the most appropriateness for you. But be aware that there are many foods that will interrupt your life cycle, that will actually get in the way of a long, strong life, and your body knows what they are. You have used in the past what you would call the testing of the muscles, you have named kinesiology. These are ways that the body can actually signal to you what it is allergic to, what it wants, what it does not want, the proper diets. If you will listen to that and use some of these tests, your body can actually communicate with you in a way to allow you to eat properly and for your own energy.

Q: Is there sin, and could you discuss the concept of sin?

A: Discussing what you would call the concept of sin has been done many times, and you know that I will say this, and it is controversial to almost all that you have been taught: There is no such thing. Sin has been and is created by human beings wishing then to assign something to it. It is often then control. It is often then punishment. For you will have some guru tell you what is appropriate and inappropriate to God and thereby control what your life might do. Sin therefore is nothing that exists on the other side of the veil. And what you might say to that is, "there must be inappropriate behavior." When you see those who are in prison for certain acts that are atrocious, when you see those who take lives, you would say, "surely that is inappropriate." And I will say to you, that is exactly what it is in the scheme of the balance you have chosen to create as your culture.

But spiritually it follows a pattern where those who have done it have done it by free choice, as part of the test of the planet. And when they get to the other side of the veil, there is no judgment. Therefore sin by the very nature of its definition does not exist as sin. There are no sins—that is to say, things you do that you will then be punished for. Let the inappropriate and appropriate behavior be set by the energy level of the planet and be then weighed with the integrity and the love that you say is your reality.

Q: Could you leave us with some uplifting words?

A: I always have uplifting words. My partner has been accused of being the "Pollyanna channel." This is a criticism that would say that "all you do is see the silver lining in all things. You say there is no hell, there is no sin. It seems that you would float because there are no empirical truths. It seems like you have no sense of right and wrong." All of these things, I will tell you, that is in the purview of the perception of the human being who has been told by others what is and what is not right and wrong. If you lift the veil and start to see all that is here, what you're going to see is pure love.

And what you're going to see within that is an uplifting potential spirit. Not only for you, but for those around you.

Your life will change dramatically at that point at which you decide to eliminate drama, hook up to that which we have called the connection to the other side of the veil, and I want you to know this, dear human being: It doesn't matter what religion you are on the planet. You can still be that and love God in this way. No matter what the doctrine is on the planet, you can still be that and love God in this way.

> The core issue . . . is that you always have been and always will be in control of your life as a piece of God in this universe. And so it is.

This is not climbing out of one box into another. This is discovering the core issue. And that is that you always have been and always will be in control of your life as a piece of God in this universe. And so it is.

≡

As Lee returned to us and rubbed his eyes, I felt light-headed, almost dizzy, as if I were in a way coming out of being in a trance myself. I could barely speak as I excused myself to the restroom to try and gather myself.

Something had happened to me in that room, in Matt's little one-bedroom apartment in the heart of Hollywood. A healing, a deep connection? I'm still not sure exactly what to call it. And I was also reeling about Kryon's revelation that I had been targeted to make the documentary and he'd have said "no" to any other person on the planet Earth.

I didn't feel pride, coming from a place of ego, but rather overwhelmed with some grand combination of gratitude, awe and, yes, love.

After my goodbye and thanks to Lee, Matt took him to the train station.

◈

As I drove home, my body was buzzing. I still felt wound up, replaying over and over what had just happened. When I arrived home, though it was only early evening, I lay on the bed and tried to court slumber. But sleep would not come. Two hours later, I had still not decompressed—my brain continuing to hula-hoop.

I got up and did other things until finally, in the shadowy wee hours, I hit the mattress again. I wondered if Kryon was "watching" me that very moment. Were the others, the ones who all seemed like old friends—Tobias, the Pleiadians, Torah, Chief Joseph, and Bashar—were they all connected to me by this invisible cord of oneness? Right now, right this moment in my little L.A. apartment?

I can't say I felt them overtly or that I heard audible voices or anything of the sort. But when I asked the question—were they around?—my heart whispered to me . . . "Of course."

Seven

Go In Peace

It's now been two years since I conducted that last interview with Kryon. The movie didn't garner a theatrical release, but it did end up being viewed by people in more than thirty countries via DVD sales. Reaction to the film has been overwhelmingly positive, and many emailed to thank us for offering up this profound fare. It was truly my pleasure, I always answered.

I am still utterly amazed at how all six nonlocal entities, though from different realms and dimensions, seemed to almost speak with one voice, each making the same points from slightly different angles. I sometimes can feel the energies of each and every one of them—and I still go to a quiet place inside and ask for guidance.

The making of the film has been a truly blessed experience that has helped me in myriad ways. Yet my life has not magically transformed. True, I have risen from my self-imposed bed of nails . . . but the new mattress, while certainly more pleasing, still sometimes feels lumpy. I cannot claim a constant state of joy just yet, so I am obviously still working out a few "core issues and beliefs," as Bashar puts it. I am pretty happy most of the time and have achieved at least a semblance of balance and harmony, but I certainly can't say that all my dreams have come true, all my yearnings have been satisfied, all my questions have been answered.

Much negativity and strife in my life have been transmuted or healed thanks to the guidance I've received from channeled material. And I feel *so* strongly about getting these messages out to lots of people that I've directed a second film, uber-creatively titled *Tuning In 2*, with seven different channelers and new topics. This work truly feels like a "calling" to me.

And yet it's one thing to listen to all the wisdom pouring forth from spirit and quite another to actually live the enlightened life in every moment, to *own* one's divinity. That *is* the true mission after all—nothing short of finally and fully realizing that, as Tobias puts it, "You are God also."

I know many of you have read oodles of spiritual books, taken the seminars, watched the uplifting movies, prayed to the gods, meditated, communed with crystals, tithed, visualized, affirmed, incanted, shrieked at the heavens, and maybe even sacrificed a goat or two. You perhaps have made incremental progress, a breakthrough or two. And yet . . . where is the true glory?

The little things are supposed to be enough—licking an ice cream cone, hugging your child, watching a sunset—and actually, they often are. And yet there is the almost constant murmur from a back room of my mind—and maybe you can relate—telling me that I am Great and that I have come to this planet to make majestic footprints. Maybe you have heard similar whispers and never really believed or acted on them. Maybe you long ago sealed off that room because it was just too painful to hear that notion of grandeur yet have nothing much to show for it. In the face of the world's brutalities and your own sense of smallness, your strength gave out and your heart gave in. Feeling gouged and gored, a futility grew over you like moss. You maybe even settled for the quietly desperate life. It's called "Divine Discontent," and for many of us it is a key step in our growth. It doesn't necessarily *have* to be that way, but often it's the path we choose on some level to wake ourselves up.

Your Greatness is still there, locked away, shackled in that room. You are only as fractured and broken as you perceive yourself to be. Some might suggest that the notion of us being great, even Godlike(!), is simply the ego being tricky. It isn't. We innately know we are Great. Infinity dances in our veins. But the world—or rather, mass consciousness—grinds this blazing thought down until it is nothing more than useless dust that blows off in the chilly breeze. Bills and obligations and "shoulds" and crappy jobs and bad marriages and cable news shows and the line at the DMV and all the rest of it often whittle us from mighty redwoods to feckless wood chips. "The world" will rip the bones from your back and steal the nose right from under your eyes if you let it.

Even now, when the entities speak of this vaunted Great Shift we have entered, the transition period to a new, more equitable and peaceful society, it can be hard not to doubt that. At times it can feel as if we are still rooted like trees to the same old, tired spot. Soldiers' blood continues to seep into the battleground, children starve, Gaia is still being raped.

go in peace 209

Sometimes it seems as if there is scant hope for mankind, that we humans are basically just shaved apes. In our pettiness and ignorance and avarice, we clumsily lurch along, rarely seeing the shimmering beauty all around us, and certainly not in our own eyes as we gaze in the mirror.

Religion tells us we are born in sin, little more than gum on the sole of God's clomping shoe. Parents teach us that the world is a dangerous and even evil place, and many of us take on this fear-based worldview by the time we are out of diapers. Popular entertainment shows us that the streets verily rush with blood. The only way to get ahead is through brutal competition in which the winners sleep between gilded sheets while much of the world shivers in the cold.

In many ways, life on Earth is nothing short of insane. We are baffled kings and ghost-eyed queens; princes wandering in a hazy mist and princesses with dented tiaras. The "American Dream" is screaming. And yet . . .

There is a faint scent of lovely lilac wafting from just over the next hill, gently beckoning us toward the promise of something grand. Maybe a few tests and trials and initiations lie between us and what's over that hill, but the lure is so enticing that we inch forward. Just exactly what lies ahead no one can say with certainty. But we *are* in the nascent stages of this Great Shift. We are slowly pecking ourselves out of the eggshell of ignorance. The chrysalis has cracked and shy light peeks through. The lilac scent reaches our nostrils and we breathe it in, a tonic. We take another step and another toward this something, this thing just out of sight. We pray that it's not another dead end, another heartless mirage.

This time it isn't.

Our family called "humanity" is just beginning to wake up from a long, brutish nightmare. We are all bearers of seeds of change, as we have been at other times, in other incarnations on Earth. But then we ended up scarecrows face down in the dirt, and those seeds blew off. Our seeds have now found purchase in the nutrient-rich soil of the new Earth we are creating with a sometimes-shaky but absolutely renewed human spirit.

And New Energy from our helpers, like the channeled entities, assists us in watering the seeds that are taking root and will sprout sweet green. How lovely and fragrant the plant becomes is strictly up to us. This transition period can be as smooth or as rough as we choose. There is a huge bulge of energy forming, but it's our responsibility to work the potter's wheel and mold things to our liking. We need to let our imaginations soar to new heights and truly become the "nation of magi" we were meant to be. We've bought into the lie of our smallness and repeatedly sold ourselves short. In our hearts we need a little more poetry and a little less salesmanship.

We poured ourselves into these bubbles of biology and chose to be here at this momentous time on the planet. We are beginning to hold more divine Light and, despite outward appearances, are remaking the world. We are pregnant with our higher selves. The birth may not be entirely pleasant . . . but the baby *is* coming. We are beginning to dream a new dream and soon the world gains more magic, like when Dorothy was carried off to Oz by that tornado and the Technicolor kicked in. We have been plowed under time and time again . . . but this time we make it over the rainbow.

We have to be our own heroes because there is no savior galloping in to save the day. Sorry, Rapture crowd. And the apostles of doom won't get their Armageddon either . . . at least not in the version of Earth I'm choosing to cocreate. Maybe next time, martyrs. Jesus is not going to part the clouds and glide down to make everything peachy. Alien spaceships will not be beaming you up and off to a better planet. And in 2012, the world won't end. Or, for that matter, magically morph into an Eden. That's the bad news, I suppose, at least for some—since all those scenarios are in a sense easy, and don't require any inner work.

The good news is that the little green bud of new life blooms lotus-like in all our hearts during this Great Awakening. The world sometimes does seem like it is engulfed in tumult and confusion . . . which is why it's so important to start listening to the whispers of spirit. What does the shouting, stumbling world know anyway? It's just an old, entrenched paradigm we've been living over and over again. And—look around—it's crumbling.

So now we do our necessary housecleaning. We shake the rugs and the air becomes heavy with dust, so dense, perhaps, that we can barely see at times. We wheeze and wander. But not to worry . . . it all settles.

You are going to have to face your inner darkness, the deep wounds, sooner or later. That is the true work here. The most fundamental "lightwork" is not to help others, but to confront the aspects maybe you don't want to look at and *heal yourself*. All else is secondary. You *will* help others in the process, but that's only a corollary. Tend to healing your own pernicious wounds, and the rest falls into place. I do speak from experience.

My own life might be considered something of a "failure" by a random observer: Dismal professional career. No family of my own. No nest egg. About twenty straight years of seeming haplessness. Two decades of scouring the backstreets of my soul, though it wasn't always at all clear *what* I was really up to. My peers cruised past me in Ferraris while I puttered along the slow lane in an old VW Bug with bald tires. I couldn't fit into the established order of things and concluded that there was something terribly wrong with me. There wasn't. I was in the midst of a profound healing for all those years.

I took myself off the cross, to use a metaphor from the religion of my youth, and resurrected. I ultimately followed Tobias's advice and became a sovereign being, got over all the rest. Or most of it, anyway.

I am still sometimes flummoxed about exactly how and *why* I have created certain events in my life, but if I follow the bread crumbs of belief I can usually arrive at a satisfactory answer. And I certainly do now believe Chief Joseph when he says that we are creating it all for ourselves, "every bit," from birth to death. It always comes down (or better yet, "rises up") to our own vibration, our frequency. If you want a mansion and it isn't appearing, don't bitterly blame the cruel world. Rather, examine your own core beliefs until your vibration matches the desire. You change your life by changing how you feel and think. That, simply, is how it works. Simple, but not always easy.

I will admit that my lack of gobs of money still sometimes confuses and even irks me. Money is fun. I like money. But I am evidently still working out the kinks in my own abundance consciousness, as I know many of you are. In the meantime, can we truly be royalty without the castle and moat, sans the jewel-filled larder? Of course we can. Because the true crown rests in the heart, not on the head. Besides, I ultimately subscribe to Tobias's view: It really doesn't matter. It would be fun to play with big piles of money, but lucre isn't necessary for joy. Our deepest desires are not material (houses, cars, cash) or power-based (control over others, winning at all costs). They are more attuned to the joy of being and true creativity. Because then we are in touch with our divinity, and it has very little to do with whether our coffers are swollen.

So, this Great Shift is not about scoring a bigger house and fancier car; in some ways it's even about getting *beyond* this bling-obsessed cultural genuflection to material things. It's about expanding consciousness . . . in fact, as the Pleiadians and others point out, taking it beyond any place it's ever been.

Take pride in that, seed-bearer. Out of billions of planets, ours is the *only one* based purely on free will, say the entities. "The test," Kryon calls it. The test of what we will do with it. It feels like we collectively are not exactly acing that exam right now . . . but we can.

As hard as it was for me driving through that darkness on the edge of town for all those years, I now realize that I on some level chose it all, wanted to totally immerse myself in some dungeons and take myself to those bloody places. I wanted to know this dense earthly experience deeply, from the inside out. I have had my teeth knocked down my throat and endured more disappointments than I care to catalog, many of my dreams left for dead on the side of the highway like roadkill. Often this planet seemed like a four-letter world, and even staying on it was a struggle.

Thankfully I never caved to the Sam route. With lots of help and guidance, I slogged through the thorny patches. Even as a sovereign being, you don't have to go it alone; we are receiving a climactic cosmic push. There is always help, if only you ask for it.

The result for me has been some sort of burnished wisdom and perhaps a certain credibility to spread the messages of these channelers. To help others get through the dark jungle underbrush at which I've already hacked away. I still have many steps to take on my own journey of self-mastery, and in fact there is really no end, no final goal to any of this. Chief Joseph's definition of success now makes more sense to me. "The true measure of success is the amount of joy you feel," he says. I've come to know that it's about life itself, each moment, and that the only real answer, trite as it may sound, is love. And there has been a certain beautiful, jagged symmetry to my path. Or maybe even that is too mystical. My journey has really been about examining those core beliefs and raising frequency.

> *Even as a sovereign being, you don't have to go it alone; we are receiving a climactic cosmic push.*

Matt also has been altered by channeling and his participation in the project. "With some hindsight, it's very obvious to me that I was 'supposed' to get involved in the movie," he says. "It all felt so right, from that first meeting over a burger with David through all the interviews, the travel, the editing. In terms of ease and everything coming together so naturally, it's by far the most amazing project I've worked on.

"But beyond that, this experience has taught me, or

at least is beginning to teach me, what's really important in life. After the shoot, I began to get rid of all the clutter in my life, whether physical or relationship-wise. I even started to question my 'Hollywood' ambitions and whether I really wanted to make the sorts of vapid movies that are generally churned out by mainstream Hollywood. My appetite for playing the games they play there diminished, and I've become much more interested in developing as a human being, sovereign and independent, while I'm here on the planet.

"I can't really say which channeler or entity affected me most, because it all seems like a perfect mosaic, a jigsaw puzzle that had to fall into place exactly like it did. But I will say that this notion of 'You are God also,' espoused by Tobias—and really all the rest of them too—has taken hold of me at some deep level. I can't say I can really wrap myself around the notion just yet, but I can feel somewhere inside that, yes, it's true. I guess I'm still figuring out, though, how to live it every day."

As am I. It's a profound idea . . . yet I realize that many of you read this sort of book to learn how to manifest bulging bank accounts, larger houses, and shiny new rides, and not necessarily for the grand pronouncements. Manifest away. You are a creator. So call forth whatever you want and play, play, play. I too like material things. I don't care to live like a cave-dwelling hermit (though I *am* quite sure I've done that in another life or two). But there is certainly more going on here—and with us—than mere measly manifestation of material things. It truly is about awareness, consciousness, and Light. It is, ultimately, about love: of self, of each other, of the planet itself.

Even some science nerd named "Einstein" recognized

this. "A human being is part of the whole called by us 'universe', a part limited in time and space," he said. "He experiences himself, his thoughts and feelings as something separated from the rest—a kind of optical illusion of his consciousness.

"This delusion is a kind of prison for us, restricting us to our personal desires and to affection for only a few persons nearest to us. Our task must be to free ourselves from this prison by widening our circle of compassion and to embrace all living creatures and the whole of nature in its beauty."

In other words, to be in love, with the world, each other, and especially ourselves. We must secede from the union of limitation and become a sovereign nation of light unto self with only one tenet in the Constitution: love. Let kindness be our new currency, our new clothes stitched with grace.

We will certainly hit a few potholes on Transition Road, maybe a hairpin turn or two, but you are the one who *chose* to come to Earth at this time and participate in this monumental shift. Don't be afraid to take the wheel, even if you don't know exactly where the car is headed, even if the sky is dark with dust and seemingly starless. The night's busted open and these two lanes will take us anywhere. Just keep the faith that you're headed in the right direction and let your headlights, dim as they may seem at times, illumine the sometimes narrow, icy road.

It all, in a sense, is just a game, a Grand Game, anyway. One you bravely came down to play, one that seems so real most of the time that you forgot it was supposed to be fun. Even without the beachfront property and the new convertible, it's supposed to be fun. As Kryon points out, we are all donning masks at the costume party. The entities say we have now fully explored all the roles, worn black hat and white, been sinner and saint. The next step is integrating it all and creating through spiritual alchemy something brand-new, something that encompasses polarity—dark and light—but goes beyond.

We have often placed ourselves in dungeons and treated each other shabbily. Well, worse really: we have killed each other. Now the game of "might is right," "greed is good," and "dog eat dog" has grown stale. The Awakening we have entered is about realizing that we don't have to do it the old way anymore; we don't have to keep pretending we're separate. We no longer need to pretend we are powerless victims knocked about by the Fates or, worse, let's face it, a pretty awful and neurotic God.

Underneath the disappointments and betrayals and scar tissue thick as a pancake, underneath it all, do you know what we *really* are? Nothing short of divinity in the flesh. Earth Angels. Yes, even the ultimate: "God also." This is what we are awakening to. So rub the sleep out of your eyes and don't hit the snooze button yet again. Rise and, well, shine. Literally. You *are ready*, or you wouldn't be reading these very words.

None of the channeled entities are more powerful than we are. Let's be clear: We are making it possible to have heaven on Earth, though since we are in the embryonic stages it perhaps doesn't exactly seem like nirvana just yet. Our nonphysical friends have answered our call to remind us of who we really are, yes, but *we* are the ones who are melding flesh and spirit, that are becoming human lighthouses. We are realizing all our self-imposed prisons have only shadows for bars.

The New Game has begun and this time we play nicer. The future is a blank page, and for not much longer will we dip our pens into blood-filled inkwells. This time, this glorious time on this glorious gift of a planet, we write in light.

About the Author

Former journalist David Thomas stumbled on channeling about a decade ago and, after delving into the phenomenon, decided to make a documentary about the subject. The result was the well-received 2009 film entitled "Tuning In." Now at work on the sequel, Thomas believes channeled material answers in profound and meaningful ways some of life's most basis yet elusive questions: Why are we here? and How can we create fulfilling lives for ourselves. The native Minnesotan now lives in Santa Barbara, where he likes to play basketball, swim in the ocean and pet random dogs. Tuning In, the movie, is at *http://www.tuninginmovie.com*.

Matthiew Klinck was raised in the small town of Aylmer, Quebec. His filmmaking began in his teens with a documentary about his grandfather's charity, and he continues to pursue this passion. A strong believer in globalism, he travels as much as possible, and presently lives in Nha Trang, Vietnam.